I0766488

FADING

TO

BLACK

How the Drug Epidemic
Was Created to Destroy
the American Middle
Class

TIMOTHY WADE CORDER

*This book is dedicated to my dear friends
who perished in this war against America's youth:*

*Jonathan Michael Horton (2010)
Christopher Scott Wong (2012)
Trent Aaron Johnson (2018)*

*To the victims of this attack
who struggle to survive today*

*And to the countless American families whose
lives have been forever changed by this epidemic.*

CONTENTS

Social Engineering:
The Driving Force of Destruction

In order to combat the devastating death and destruction brought to the citizens of our nation by drug addiction, particularly in recent years, it's important to have a clear understanding of how this situation has evolved—or rather, how it was *orchestrated* as part of a war against the American middle class. Yes, as citizens of this great nation, we are victims of twenty-first century psychological warfare. Unlike traditional wars in which we've lost our bright, talented sons and daughters in foreign lands, they're dying right here on American soil—on our streets, in our Emergency Departments, in the restrooms of gas stations and fast food restaurants, and in many cases even in our own homes.

As the casualties continue to come in at an alarming pace, it's time to stop looking at the tens of thousands of senseless tragedies as if they were somehow self-induced. It's time to stop blaming ourselves for ineffective parenting or fundamental problems intrinsic to our society for the fact that this nightmare is becoming a reality for so many

American families. It's time to get angry and fight back against the forces that are responsible for reducing thousands of children and young adults to bittersweet memories and tragic statistics. It's time to launch a strategic defense initiative and wage a counterattack against the global elites and their social engineers.

The drug epidemic, including the opioid crisis, did not simply appear as an organically occurring phenomenon. It is not the product of randomly occurring trends or coincidences, nor does it represent any sweeping character deficits that exist among those who have fallen prey to it. In the following pages, we will demonstrate the deliberate, baneful, and unconscionable manner in which this epidemic was synthesized as a direct attack against the United States of America by some of the world's most powerful and influential people whose end goals are to weaken, destabilize, and ultimately destroy our culture by transforming us into a nation of addicts. It is their hope that we will become so weak, so dependent, and so distracted that we'll fail to stand against the obliteration of our society and the subversion of our God-given rights. We will identify the key players, discuss the motivating factors behind their utter depravity, and describe the many social engineering tactics they have employed to further their objectives.

In my 2019 book, *War for Your Worldview: What Every American Needs to Know in the Age of Fake News, Social Engineering, and Mind-Controlling Propaganda*, I introduce readers to a powerful, elite cabal that consists of three hundred of the world's wealthiest and most influential bankers, businessmen, politicians, and members of royal nobility who quietly run the world from behind the scenes. Among them are various factions and sub-groups (e.g., the Club of Rome, the Bilderberg Group, the Olympians, the Council on Foreign Relations, et. al.) that hold private meetings around the globe to discuss geopolitics, attempt to reach consensus with regard to public policies, and collaborate about how to steer the nations of the world and all of its inhabitants toward a totalitarian political and economic system over which they, and they alone, enjoy absolute power and control.

There is a seemingly endless list of names that have been used to identify these groups, including the "Illuminati," the "Order of Skull and Bones," the "Freemasons," and more recently the "Establishment," and the "Deep State" to name just a few. Rest assured, the confusion created by having multiple, interconnected groups whose memberships overlap is intentional. It's meant to diffuse responsibility, exasperate investigators, and create ambiguity, all of which are skills they have mastered.

In this book I refer to them as the Committee of 300 and by two other more general terms that I use interchangeably: the "elites" and the "globalists." Why? It's more accurate than using the ever-changing group names that they can shed like snakeskin any time they fear retaliation from an increasingly aware and angry public. Furthermore, the names they choose can be quite misleading and are often sanitized so the public will not only find them more palatable but also believe their missions are noble and philanthropic.

None of these groups is inclusive of everyone involved in the global conspiracy which has survived through many generations of participants who have hailed from every continent and are all, to varying degrees, committed to the world government agenda. For example, not everyone who attended Bilderberg meetings also sat on the Council on Foreign Relations (CFR), which, coincidentally, has a name that sounds innocent enough, right? To unsuspecting people of good will who have faith in the altruistic intentions of their government, the name would likely bring to mind a panel of highly ethical and morally upstanding officials who convene to exchange important ideas about America's thoughtful and responsible interactions with other nations. Anyone who is familiar with the CFR's history and the goals shared among its members, however, knows that it is a corrupt, lawless team of wealthy socialites who are committed to subverting the founding principles of the United States of America. Of course, "Council on Foreign Relations," draws less public scrutiny and looks much better on official letterhead than "Rogue Panel of Anti-American Scoundrels." But I digress.

It seems appropriate to refer to them using terms that brand them as accurately as possible. We should call them who and what they actually are--elite globalists who have only two universally identifying characteristics 1) massive wealth which is used to exert influence on the public, and 2) commitment to merging the nations of the world to form a single, totalitarian regime at the expense of individual freedom and prosperity. Some will be mentioned by name. Readers who are interested in a complete list of those who sit on the Committee of 300, however, are directed to the Appendix of my aforementioned book.

Although there has always been a certain amount of discourse and infighting among the elites about which path to take toward their final destination, their fundamental objective to impose a world government/economic system consisting of a slave labor class (us) and an elite ruling class (them) has been agreed upon for more than a century. The enormous wealth held by these individuals has allowed them to wield power by infiltrating and commandeering powerful roles within government agencies, corporations, academia, the scientific community, and news and entertainment media outlets. They fill these positions with operatives who are loyal to their interests, not ours, and use bribery and intimidation tactics to keep the corruption alive and well at the top levels of social, political, and economic hierarchies.

As members inevitably die and new people are recruited into their inner circles, the names and faces of the elites change slightly. At their core, however, they remain unchanged—their arrogance, their pompous disregard for the rights and welfare of their fellow human beings, and their participation in egregious acts against people who have never done them an iota of harm. The stranglehold they maintain on practically every institution via their expansive spheres of influence has been directly responsible for immeasurable human suffering. They've deliberately created famines, diseases, and disasters, and funded both sides of conflicts between nations to cause wars in which millions of innocent souls have perished.

The elites tend to meet in secret and discuss their plans in private groups, but their actions are carried out in broad daylight where they hide in plain view. Sadly, they often proceed with enormous support from public groups who have been hoodwinked into believing they're working for "do-gooders" who are guided by efforts to create a better world. It's eerily reminiscent of how the Nazis charged their victims, who willingly paid, train fare to the death camps.

In this book, I proceed with the presumption that the reader has a general understanding of the world's power structure, particularly as it relates to the pervasive and omnipresent influence imposed by the elites, their unflinching malevolence, and the depths to which they have enabled themselves to reach into virtually every aspect of our lives—their agenda relying largely on their mastery of deception and the exploitation of our most noble qualities for use against us. Through the introduction of carefully crafted propaganda, divisive and emotionally-charged rhetoric, and well established, reliable mind control tactics, they have succeeded at shaping our values, manipulating our thought processes, and ultimately directing the trajectory of our society to align with their desired outcomes. The globalists have used multi-faceted approaches to invade our collective psyche, but in this book the scope is narrowed to provide a detailed look at how our nation has been attacked with deadly drugs, particularly opioid drugs, and how the cycles of addiction have been perpetuated, promoted, and protected to compromise American strength, stability and sovereignty, all while profits from the drug trade have further enriched the enemy.

A conceptual trap that people can easily fall into is the belief that the dreaded elite power grab will occur at some point in the future and will involve an earth-shaking, cataclysmic event that facilitates the rich and powerful taking over the world. Let me be very clear. The doomsday scenario that many have spent years planning and preparing for is already upon us. Our destruction has been ongoing, all the while accelerating, for decades. Make no mistake—

despite victories and setbacks on both sides of this struggle, the elite ruling class has already, by and large, seized control over most aspects of the human experience. It's now entirely up to us to decide how much more ground we will allow them to gain. May this book empower the reader to stand against the oppressors who are fiercely determined to destroy the gifts of life, free will, and the spirit of human resilience that were so graciously bestowed upon us by God.

Arthur Thomson, a highly respected historian and the author of the 2017 book *To the Victor Go the Myths and Monuments*, identified the core principles the elites are guided by in their quest to destroy Western civilization, particularly the United States, to bring all nations under the control of world government:[1]

- the overthrow of all governments,
- the destruction of religion,
- the abolition of private property,
- the death of individualism and family,
- the deification of sensuality (hedonism),
- the repudiation of marriage,
- the state control of children, and
- the establishment of a world government.

Drugs are, of course, a fundamental component of hedonism, and indulgence in them has been pushed with the knowledge that the erosion of a society can be accomplished more easily if our attention is consumed with doing what feels good rather than what's actually good for us. While distracting us with drugs, mindless entertainment, and the superficial pleasures of promiscuity, the elites have used broadcast media to phase out religious values, particularly those of Christianity, encouraging us to replace morality with a carefree "anything goes" mentality.

We've been warned that drugs are illegal and that using them will negatively impact our health and relationships until they ultimately destroy our lives. At the same time, the drug culture has been propped up and glamorized to bait us into experimentation that ultimately leads to addiction—a classic "double-bind" paradox that's rooted in the notion that "forbidden fruit is sweeter."

We've certainly seen the destruction, not only in the surge of overdose deaths, but also in terms of disability. Drugs are transforming us into a society that's becoming less capable, as evidenced by the fact that only 29 percent of eighteen year-old Americans are now qualified to enter the U.S. armed forces.[2] The other 71 percent are rejected due to addiction, related criminal history, or other physical limitations such as obesity. Without bold action on our part, there's no reason to believe that these trends are going to reverse themselves anytime soon.

Much of the factual information we have that connects the globalists to specific events that mark the inception of the drug counter-culture in the U.S. and Europe was exposed by world renowned author, former Russian Intelligence Agent, and Nobel Prize Laureate, Dr. Daniel Estulin. Some of his best-selling books include, "*In the Shadows pf a Presidency*," *The Tavistock Institute, The True Story of the Bilderberg Group, Social Engineering of the Masses*, and *Shadow Masters*. In Chapters 2 and 4, we explore some of the facts he and other researchers have unearthed for us. We begin, however, with the hard facts that emphasize the scale of the drug crisis in the U.S.

Americans rarely consider the possibility of outside forces invading our homeland. The U.S. military is a force so formidable that no leader in his or her right mind would dare to lead an attack on America's mainland. If such a scenario were ever to occur, however, in such a way that civilians were confronted, would the American people go quietly? Although a handful might, I believe that the majority of us would fight with unparalleled resolve to defend our homes, our families, and our property. So, it's quite ironic that when our homes are invaded nightly through the television, our children are under attack daily in their classrooms, and the weapon used is just as powerful and deadly as anything ever encountered on a battlefield, we not only capitulate, but actively participate in our own demise.

America is, indeed, *Fading to Black*, the title chosen as the word "black" is a common street name for heroin, and the bright light that once illuminated our shining city on the hill is fading fast. It's time to see this crisis for what it truly is, rise up, and defend ourselves as if our lives depended on it. As very disturbing trends and statistics suggest, they do.

CHAPTER 1

A Nation on its Knees: Recent Trends and Statistics

Deaths from unintentional opiate overdoses have doubled since the year 2013 and more than quadrupled since 2000.[3] In 2017, more Americans between the ages of 20 and 34[4] were killed by opiates than in motor vehicle crashes.[5] During that same year a total of 72,000 (approximately the population of Gulfport, Mississippi) Americans perished from accidental drug overdoses, which set a new national record. Of those, approximately 46,000 lives were claimed by synthetic opioids[6]. That's more casualties in one year than we experienced throughout the course of the Vietnam War.

A 2018 study that appeared in the *Journal of the American Medical Association* found that close to 9,000 children and teenagers have died from opiate overdoses over the past 2 decades. In fact, the death rate from heroin and other opiate overdoses is so high that it's now driving down the average life expectancy for citizens of the United States and is the number one cause of accidental death among people under the age of eighteen.[7] Although men and women of all ages are included in these grim numbers, the epidemic is affecting men at a ratio of nearly two to one, and of those men, the majority are under the age of thirty-four.

The backdrop for addiction to opiates and other deadly drugs has changed dramatically in recent years. What was once a problem that seemed limited to the inner cities and often involved the stereotypical "hippies," minority groups, and disenfranchised veterans, has spread outward from the cities to the suburbs, reaching into rural, predominantly white, middle-class communities. Overdose deaths from heroin and prescription opiates have been increasing at alarming rates across America's heartland, particularly in states like Michigan, Ohio, Kentucky, West Virginia, and Pennsylvania—places where the post-industrial outsourcing of jobs and the closing of once thriving factories and mines has led to feelings of helplessness, despair, and pain, from which these powerful drugs have allowed people a way to temporarily escape. There are now more than 2 million Americans who use opiate drugs on a daily basis, and that number is growing.[8]

As the demand for drugs increases, so does the potency of the products users are getting. This makes sense given that stronger drugs can be transported and stored in smaller spaces—a major advantage to dealers and smugglers who wish to avoid detection. The synthetic opiate drug, fentanyl, which has been implicated in more than 100,000 overdose deaths in the U.S. since 2005,[9] is twenty-five to fifty times stronger than heroin. More recently, its powerful successor, carfentanyl, which is up to 100 times stronger than fentanyl, is being seized by police and DEA agents around the country with increasing frequency. Both drugs are so potent that exposure to as little as one milligram can be fatal.

The United States consumes a whopping 80 percent of the opiates produced throughout the world despite the fact that Americans only account for approximately 4.1 percent of the world population.[10] As a result, an average of 175 Americans die from overdoses every single day.[11] If terror attacks were killing 175 people per day, imagine the swift and effective response our government would unleash. The lives claimed represent people of every age, racial, and socioeconomic group. Thousands of children are also impacted by this epidemic each year, many becoming orphans when their parents overdose and die, some losing their parents to the corrections system because of drug related charges, and others simply becoming addicted themselves. The average American does, in fact, appear to be keenly aware of the harm caused by this epidemic. A 2018 poll found that 90 percent of adults who live in rural areas report that opiate addiction is "a serious problem" in their communities.12

Dr. Ken Harshbarger oversees the Montgomery County Coroner's office that serves the city of Dayton, Ohio. He describes the nightmare that has unfolded in his jurisdiction, which was recently ranked the number one city in America for overdose deaths. His facility, once adequate to serve the needs of the community, is equipped to store up to eight bodies while autopsies and toxicology tests are performed. He recalls a time when the space and the small staff that supports his work were sufficient. Recent trends have started to change all of that.

His office is now operating above capacity almost every day. Some days it becomes necessary to rotate those who are awaiting disposition as there are not enough refrigerated units to hold them all at the same time. His staff and the modest budget he operates on are also stretched to their limits. He simply does not have the resources, the manpower, or the space needed to respond to the growing number of casualties that are constantly arriving. Tragically, he notes that many of the decedents who are subjects of his investigations are under the age of thirty. Some are under eighteen.[13]

Local paramedics who serve this area are so inundated with calls to help overdose victims that the local sheriff's deputies have started carrying naloxone in their vehicles so they can respond to 911 calls with this life-saving intervention. This became necessary as emergency medical personnel have often been so busy with other overdose calls that they simply cannot reach everyone who needs help in time.[14] In nearby Stark County, the local coroner has been forced to request refrigerated mobile morgue units to be sent from the state capital in Columbus to accommodate the dead--the specialized vehicles that are built and kept on hand for use in the event of a major accident or natural disaster that results in mass casualties.[15]

In West Virginia, a state with a long history of economic challenges and a total population of just above one million people, there were 780 million hydrocodone and oxycodone pills distributed in 2016. In a small town in the southern part of the state, there were more than 3 million oxycodone pills shipped to a local pharmacy during a ten month period in 2017--or about 10,000 pills per day! Something has to be terribly wrong for this to occur in a town with only 400 residents.16 In Huntington, West Virginia, the Director of Emergency Services for Cabell County told an interviewer that her department responds to an average of five overdose calls every day. She went on to say that she cannot remember the last time a day went by without at least one. Nearly 5 percent of babies born in West Virginia are addicted to opiates at birth, a number that has tripled since 1999.17

West Virginia is said to be at the epicenter of the opiate epidemic. In 2018 the death rate for opiate overdose was 43.4 per 100,000 population—more than triple the national average.18 The problem has prompted West Virginia and a handful of other state governments to file claims against Purdue and other pharmaceutical manufacturers for damages, including punitive damages from companies accused of willfully suppressing information they knew about their products' addictive properties.19 As the epidemic continues to strain state budgets and exhaust local resources, it seems likely that other states will soon follow suit.

Many of these statistics are from data gathered before 2019. Data collected during the last year suggests that overdose deaths from opiates are beginning to decline slightly for the first time since the onset of the epidemic nearly thirty years ago. This is believed to be due, in part, to the fact that more people are now able to acquire the emergency drug Naloxone for use in their homes.[20] This shouldn't be taken, however, as a sign that the overall problem is improving. Although the death rate has decreased slightly, the number of Americans who become addicted to these drugs continues to rise steadily.

Although the opiate crisis is an epidemic in and of itself, it's only part of America's debilitating drug problem. The use of other highly addictive drugs has also been surging in recent years. Deaths by overdose of methamphetamine and other psychostimulants reportedly increased by 21 percent between 2017 (10,749) and 2018 (12,987). Polysubstance abuse is also on the rise, as evidenced by the fact that roughly half of those who die from methamphetamine overdoses also have a detectable level of at least one opiate drug in post-mortem toxicology screenings.[21] Law enforcement seizure of methamphetamine in 2018 increased by 142 percent from 2017.[22] If the amount of meth seized has doubled, it's likely that the amount being trafficked into the U.S. has also doubled. This is an alarming trend, especially for first responders who are frequently injured attempting to calm or subdue individuals who are high on meth. The vast majority of meth that's consumed in the U.S. now comes from Mexico. Drug enforcement officers were astonished by the size of one particular operation after they raided an elaborate production lab in Mexico that was able to manufacture up to seven tons of meth per day.[23]

Cocaine use is also on the rise, the drug reportedly causing the second highest number of overdose deaths among Americans, and the highest number of overdose deaths of black Americans.[24] The fact that it's relatively easy to overdose on cocaine coupled with the drug's powerfully addictive properties makes it especially dangerous and gives rise to great concern about the growing number of users. Cocaine use has been increasing since 2010 in virtually all demographic groups.[25] Unfortunately, this problem is being overshadowed by the opioid epidemic and is therefore not getting the attention it deserves. Cocaine addiction presents unique challenges in terms of treatability, as no drug has been developed that helps patients recover or manages withdrawal symptoms.

In 2018, The National Institute on Drug Abuse found that more than 11.8 million young people in the United States reported using marijuana within the past year.[26] Daily use significantly increased among teenagers in the eighth, tenth, and twelfth grades nationwide in 2019.[27] Students' perceptions of the risks associated with marijuana have declined over the past year,[28] which might be a product of media campaigns created to soften public opinion to garner support for legalization. As many as 7 percent of high school students now report using the drug daily.[29] It's important to keep in mind, however, that the marijuana of today is not the same drug it was fifty or even twenty years ago. The pot that was grown and sold in the U.S. during the 1960s and 70s typically had a tetrahydrocannabinol (THC) content of about 2 percent. A lab in Colorado recently studied the composition of 600 samples of marijuana and found some to have a THC content as high as 30 percent.[30] Obviously such a dramatic increase in the psychoactive component of the drug results in an entirely different experience for the user.

The misconceptions of urban folklore that exist about marijuana are extensive. This is probably both a cause and an effect of the drug being legalized for recreational use in four states, and for medical use in twenty-three states. Data generally supports the conclusion that "marijuana is a gateway drug." In fact, the vast majority of heroin addicts began their drug initiation with marijuana, and as the age of first trial goes down, the likelihood of developing an addiction as an adult goes up.[31] This is not to imply that everyone who uses marijuana will go on to use "harder" drugs, but adults who are addicted to marijuana are three times more likely to be addicted to heroin than those not addicted to marijuana. It's of utmost importance that we reverse these trends in young people, as we know that the use of alcohol, marijuana, and nicotine during the teen years predisposes the brain to form addiction pathways. Sadly, in many cases, the kids who are smoking pot today will be the adults who are injecting opiates tomorrow.

The cancer of addiction has metastasized to every city, small town, and rural community in America. It has affected people from all walks of life, tearing families apart, separating children from their parents, and creating enormous demands on our already strained healthcare system. Most Americans now know at least one person who has lost a loved one to addiction. Yet, despite our best efforts, the sad stories remain all too frequent. So how did we get here? And who is to blame?

CHAPTER 2

How We Got Here and Who is to Blame

We have known for several decades that the very wealthy and powerful elite globalists operate within secret societies (e.g., Committee of 300, Bilderberg Group, Club of Rome, et. al.) that quietly rule the world. They declared war on the American middle class many years ago, believing that our strong, educated, and heavily armed citizenry and our Constitution were obstacles that stood between them and their global, "utopian" society.

Esteemed author, researcher, lecturer, Constitutional expert, and former British MI-6 intelligence agent, Dr. John Coleman, described many of the techniques these groups have employed in their attacks against our people, our Constitution, and our economic stability. In addition to outsourcing our jobs, killing our once thriving industries, and attempting to destabilize our nation through policies that encourage mass immigration of unskilled workers, they have manufactured social problems (e.g., racial conflicts, terror attacks, etc.) and used the media to enhance the fear, anger, and anxiety people feel as a result.[32]

It is by dominating the news and entertainment media, the education system, and even decisions made by our own elected officials that they are able to control the national conversation, and thus, influence the issues people feel passionately about. For example, the Rockefeller Foundation invented and introduced America and the world to the concept of feminism during the second half of the twentieth century. They did not do so out of any concern for women's rights or to eradicate sexism or gender inequality. They admittedly created the feminist movement to drive the American tax base closer to 100 percent by releasing propaganda designed to lure women into the workplace, which would also force children into daycares and public schools at younger ages, thereby ensuring their complete indoctrination.[33] Their ability to dominate popular culture by controlling much of what comes out of Hollywood and broadcast media outlets made it relatively easy for them to convince millions of women to abandon their traditional roles as wives and mothers and seek jobs outside the home. The plan, which focused on delegitimizing men and shaming the roles of traditional women was enormously successful.

Billionaire George Soros is the financial muscle of efforts to legalize drugs in the United States. Since the 1980s he has poured over $200 million into magazine ads, television productions, and various other campaigns targeting the public with propaganda aimed at softening views on legalizing marijuana. He insists that current approaches to fighting drug use are ineffective and proposes that legalization is the solution.34 While he may be correct about the failures of our efforts, his logic doesn't recognize the reason drugs are illegal in the first place—they destroy lives! Of course this is of no consequence to Soros, a high-ranking, senior member of the Committee of 300, who believes that public views and policies on drug use should be divorced from those related to crime, despite the fact that study after study confirms a direct relationship between the two.

As the father and founder of the Drug Legalization Agenda, Soros, a devout atheist, and his acolytes consistently bankroll efforts to influence public opinion and change legislative policies. He is also the founder and financier of "Open Societies," which pushes for the dissolution of international borders of sovereign nations, particularly those of the United States and Israel. He has contributed millions of dollars to pro-abortion and pro-euthanasia causes in addition to funding black activist groups (e.g., Black Lives Matter), Antifa, and other protest groups that employ violence and intimidation tactics to spark civil unrest in the name of "social justice."[35]

When considering all of the causes Soros has provided extensive support for, some disturbing themes emerge. All are somehow either involved in shortening the lives of the American people, destroying our domestic tranquility, promoting immorality and chaos within our society, or compromising our national sovereignty. He clearly hates America and wants to fundamentally change our values. For more than 30 years, his staggering wealth and dedication to backing these causes have enabled him to do exactly that. He should be viewed as public enemy number one!

Although Soros is unquestionably the biggest drug legalization proponent of all time, he is not by any means waging this battle alone. A host of other wealthy men and corporations have also shown tremendous interest in efforts to make drugs legal in the United States. Others who have contributed heavily to the cause include Laurence Rockefeller, John Sperling, and George Zimmer, each giving over $100,000 for the initiative in California.[36] It's worth mentioning that 68 percent of the money donated to the legalization campaigns in California came from these and other out-of-state contributors,37 a fact that certainly poses the question: Whose interests are being served by elite businessmen continuously funding policy changes in states where they don't even reside?

The egregious acts of George Soros went unnoticed for many years, but his seemingly endless interference in American political and social affairs have recently earned him some attention from the U.S. Department of Justice. Attorney General William Barr blasted him in a 2019 interview with Fox News' Martha McCallum for funding the campaigns of radical left-wing district attorneys which Barr stated will result in a reduction of police and an increase in crime in those areas.38 Barr should be questioning the legality of his tendency to fund all things anti-American.

The drug culture in America is the result of subversive mind control tactics that have been employed on a massive scale to undermine our values—a sinister plot that millions of innocent Americans and citizens of other countries have been the unwitting victims of. When we consider the devastation, destruction, and loss of life that the social engineers have brought upon countless individuals and families, it should make everyone uniformly outraged.

To demonstrate that the drug epidemic was created deliberately and with malicious intent, we turn to the following passage from Dr. Coleman's book, *Conspirators Hierarchy*:

> "The war on drugs which the Bush administration is allegedly fighting, but which it is not, is for TOTAL legalization of ALL types and classes of drugs. Such drugs are not solely a social aberration, but a full-scale attempt to gain control of the minds of the people of this planet, or as the *"Aquarian Conspiracy"* authors put it, *"to bring about radical changes in the United States."* this is the principal task of the Committee of 300, the ultimate secret society."[39]

Dr. Coleman also exposed the role of the Tavistock Institute on Human Relations, the propaganda arm of the Committee of 300 that creates powerful broadcast media to influence people worldwide and to promote drugs through rock and other types of music. In fact, it was the Tavistock Institute that invented *The Beatles* in the 1960s and promoted their rise to superstardom in order to create a counter-culture centered around hallucinogenic drugs that would fascinate the minds of the young people of that era with songs like *Lucy in the Sky with Diamonds* (LSD), and others that glorified hallucinogens, thereby encouraging a generation of young Americans and Europeans to experiment with these substances.40   According to Dr. Coleman, the late John Lennon's assassination in 1981 was carried out amidst rumors that he was considering going public with the insidious agenda that he felt a deep sense of guilt for having ever been a part of.41

Anyone who believes popular music in the 1960s and 70s was the result of a naturally emerging drug culture needs to understand that it was the messages in music, invented and dictated by the elites through the Tavistock Institute, that *created* the drug culture.   Dr. Coleman points out that *The Rolling Stones* were also a brainchild of Tavistock institute, as were *The Grateful Dead*, both groups that glamorized drugs, both groups that had tremendous influence over the millions of young people who idolized them.42

We learn from the journalist, best-selling author, and former Russian Intelligence Agent, Dr. Daniel Estulin, that the historic Woodstock celebration that took place in Bethel, New York in August of 1969 was a controlled experiment conducted at the behest of the elites by CIA operatives and the Council on Foreign Relations.43   More than 400,000 teens and young adults attended the three-day concert which hosted a total of thirty-two performances by various artists including Jimi Hendrix, Janis Joplin, and Jim Morrison, all of whom boldly embodied the emerging drug culture, all of whom seemed to come out of nowhere just before becoming insanely popular overnight. Woodstock has been called a pivotal moment in music history, although the lasting stain it left on an entire generation of young people qualifies it as a pivotal moment in America's cultural decline—the birth of a rebellious counter-culture of sex, drugs, and rock n' roll. According to Estulin, LSD and other drugs were distributed freely to members of the audience who huddled in pits in the mud in altered states of consciousness as heavy rain poured down on them for three days.44

The plan is laid out quite clearly in *Bread and Circuses*, an essay originally composed by a group of French senior bankers who met in Canada in 1967 and again in 1985. This document was reportedly leaked and exposed by the Canadian journalist, Serge Monast. This relatively short but telling document is essentially a blueprint that provides intricate details of how the elites proposed to corrupt the people and demolish nation-states in the west by creating a culture of drugs and immorality while occupying the average citizen's attention with mindless activities like sporting events. Note that Adolf Hitler also used sports to distract citizens across Europe prior to WWII, and replaced religious curriculum with mandatory sports participation in schools.[45] Indeed, we've seen that many of the ideas set forth in this document, which pre-dated the Woodstock festival by only a few months, have come to fruition. An excerpt follows:

> "All historical periods that led to the decline of civilizations were marked, without exception, by 'the spirit of errancy of men.' Today, we must ensure that the 'Spirit' will result from a 'World Society of Leisure' in all its forms. This 'Leisure' should consist of sex, drugs, sport, exotic travel, and entertainment in general, but available to all strata of society…To achieve this objective it is imperative to be able to infiltrate the Media (radio, TV, newspapers), the milieu of the 'Mode' and 'Culture' (the milieu of. New music) by which we will influence, for sure, all sections of Western societies. So taking under our thumb the 'Sense' of young people (the adults of tomorrow), we will therefore open the way to infiltrate and transform profoundly, without arousing suspicion, Politics, the Legal System, and Education, which will allow us to fundamentally change the future direction of Society envisaged by our plan."[46]

The legalization of drugs is also mentioned later in the same article in a list of social problems the elites of the day intended to impose on free societies in pursuit of global enslavement and world government:

> "Thanks to the misinformation, lies, hypocrisy, and individualism that we have created among the people of Nation-States, this Man will become an enemy for humans. Thus these "Independent Individuals," who are more dangerous to us precisely because of their "Freedom," will be considered by their peers as enemies, not liberators. Child slavery, the pillaging of the Third World, unemployment, propaganda for the liberalization of anti-drug laws, the brutalization of the youth of Nations, the ideology of "Respect for Individual Freedom" diffused in Judeo-Christian Churches and within the Nation-States, obscurantism considered as a basis of pride, inter-ethnic conflicts, and our latest achievement: "Budget cuts;" with all that we can finally see the performance of our ancestral "Dream:" the introduction of our "New World Order.""

Note that every prediction in this disturbing passage is readily observable today, whether emerging or already well-established, in American society.

The notorious Tavistock Institute, which is still very active in London today, served as the link between the elite globalists' plan and the music venues of the 1960s that prompted America to spiral into addiction. If you find this level of social control to be strangely Orwellian, consider the following passage extracted directly from *1984*.

"The use of "recreational" drugs shall be compulsory, with each person allotted drug quotas which can be purchased at One World Government stores throughout the world. Mind control drugs will be expanded, and usage will become compulsory. Such mind control drugs shall be given in food and/or water supplies without the knowledge and/or consent of the people. Drug bars shall be set up, run by One World Government employees, where the slave-class shall be able to spend their free time. In this manner the non-elite masses will be reduced to the level and behavior of controlled animals with no will of their own and easily regimented and controlled."[47]

Of course, the medical community cannot escape its fair share of the responsibility for this crisis given the enormous role prescription drugs have played, particularly opiate drugs, which doctors have been accused of over-prescribing to their patients. Countless deadly addictions have started with drugs prescribed to treat pain associated with legitimate medical conditions. To be fair, many physicians who practice in today's healthcare system are finding themselves in unenviable positions. With the changes brought about by managed care, most doctors have been forced to substantially increase their caseloads which translates to a drastic reduction in the amount of time that can be spent with each patient.

Patients who visit doctors with vague complaints of pain often demand immediate solutions, but properly identifying and treating the true underlying origin of pain is often a lengthy, complex, and expensive process—one that neither patients with limited benefits nor doctors who are pressed for time can fully engage in. It's much easier to delay or circumvent the process altogether by simply treating patients with pain-killing opiate drugs. But does that mean doctors share the burdens of responsibility for this crisis? The answer is complicated.

Modern physicians are also targeted by pharmaceutical companies who invite them to lavish conferences where they're often subjected to elaborate, high-pressure sales pitches, given free drug samples, and pushed, even offered incentives, to prescribe their products. When they began to face criticism for contributing to high rates of addiction and overdose deaths, some cut their patients off or significantly reduced their prescriptions, forcing many pill addicts to find alternative sources, including the heroin sold on the streets.

No reasonable, forward-thinking person would assume that American physicians are part of a conspiracy to destroy the U.S. with prescription drugs. While there are undeniably doctors and other providers who are more concerned with profits than the well-being of their patients, they are the exception, not the rule. Most doctors hold themselves to the highest ethical standards and honor their sacred oath to "do no harm." Of course, that doesn't mean there aren't physicians in the top tiers of the medical and pharmaceutical industries whose actions are driven entirely by greed. Follow the money. The trail leads to a pyramid at the top of which you'll find the elite globalists and all of the corruption that defines them.

The medical establishment, the insurance industry, and big pharm have been referred to as the "unholy trinity," inextricably intertwined and operating in concert to enrich themselves by keeping people sick. In a 2018 article in *Global Research*, Joachim Hagopian wrote:

> "Another cold hard reality is pharmaceutical drugs especially when consumed to manage chronic disease and symptoms cause severe side effects that also damage, harm and kill. The most prescribed drugs of all are painkillers that tend to be highly addictive. Big pharm with the help of their global army of doctors have purposely and calculatingly turned a large percentage of us especially in the United States into hardcore drug addicts, both physically and psychologically addicted to artificial synthetic substances that are detrimental to our health and well-being."[48]

So, does this mean that your family doctor is part of the conspiracy to turn you into an addict? Not at all. Agan, most doctors are upstanding people who entered the medical field, at least in part, out of fascination with biological science. Most also have a genuine desire to serve people, save lives, and reduce human suffering. The representative you speak with when you call your insurance company probably also has your best interest in mind. Research scientists who work in biochemistry labs developing medications are also, by and large, people of good will who are driven by an altruistic desire to cure diseases and promote wellness through scientific discoveries. Those at the top who enjoy the enormous profits generated by these industries, however, are often driven by less honorable intentions. According to the Center for Research on Globalization:

> "Plenty of empirical evidence exists that confirm concerted diabolical efforts have been made to ruin the lives of pioneers who have come up with possible cures for cancer, AIDS and other terminal illnesses. Obviously, their work poses a serious threat to the medical status quo. Hence, their treatments have all been effectively suppressed by conventional medicine. Bottom line, if humans are healthy, the healthcare industry does not survive. Thus, it's in its own inherently self-serving interest to promote illness in the name of wellness."[49]

Meanwhile, the same people who gave us *The Beatles*, Woodstock, and Jimi Hendrix in the late 1960s were still working diligently during the 1980s and 90s to bombard us with even more hypnotic, drug-glamorizing artists and celebrities. The birth of Music Television (MTV) in 1981 was the result of thoughtful planning by the very same Tavistockian, "mass brainwashing" social engineers, "in order to reach out to young people without the society being aware of the deceit" to 'create a counter-institution that would preach values contrary to those which prevailed in the society."[50]

Of course, the federal government's response to the drug crisis has been misguided and ineffective at best. Unparalleled corruption that exists at the highest levels of the executive and legislative branches, and within the intelligence community is at least part of the reason nothing they've done has resulted in any noticeable improvement. It's clear that many who have been in power haven't wanted this epidemic to be brought under control—a bold statement that leads into the next chapter.

CHAPTER 3

The War on Drugs:
From Nixon to Trump

For almost 50 years, the United States has been engaged in what President Richard Nixon first termed "the war on drugs" which he called for in June of 1971. Although it has continued through the administrations of nine presidents, the current epidemic is evidence that the war on drugs has been an epic failure. Critics of government policies argue that approaching the drug problem by attempting to stop the supply of drugs coming into the country is ineffective in that it only serves to drive higher prices and results in the availability of drugs with higher potency.

Early attempts to limit the supply of methamphetamine in the U.S. focused on outlawing chemicals that were necessary to produce the drug. Although this forced the larger manufacturers out of business, smaller meth labs began to spring up, particularly in the western part of the country. The government responded by outlawing even more chemicals which effectively shifted control of the market to the Mexican drug cartels who were able to make more potent forms of the drug and were already experienced at smuggling across our border. The government's actions did nothing to address the demand for the drug. But by attempting to go after the supply, their actions only drove up the price and moved the task of supplying the drug into more organized, violent, and difficult to prosecute hands.[51]

Before diving into this topic, it's important to keep in mind that throughout the entire span of the war on drugs, our presidents and other elected officials have been controlled, to greater or lesser extent, by orders from the Committee of 300. With the exceptions of Reagan and Trump, all have been selected by the elite establishment which ultimately presides over both parties at the top, despite our belief that our votes represent a choice between opposing ideologies. In most of our elections, one side wins, one side loses, and "business as usual" carries on in Washington, regardless of which party prevails. Blackmail and intimidation tactics are used to control the actions of our presidents and most of our congressional representatives by way of the intelligence community and other shadow government forces whose power, unchecked and unchallenged, reigns supreme. That said, what has our government actually done with the 50 years and $1.1 trillion in taxpayer money they've spent supposedly trying to close this hemorrhaging wound? How much of what they're telling us amounts to anything more than platitudes, rhetoric, and lip service that seeks only to pacify and appease a public that has grown increasingly skeptical and ever more desperate for a practical solution? They have not only repeatedly failed to achieve any appreciable progress but continue to lose ground faster than ever before. The remainder of this chapter presents the highlights of each president's administration's positions and policies enacted under the pretense of fighting the nebulous and seemingly endless war on drugs.

Richard Nixon (Republican, 1969-1974)

When President Richard Nixon first called for the war on drugs, his declaration was seen by some as a mere political strategy to improve his odds of being elected to a second term. He was accused of weaponizing law enforcement against black voters and the "hippie" movement, both of which were groups that predominantly opposed him.[52] Although this was allegedly confirmed decades later by his counsel and Assistant for Domestic Affairs, John Ehrlichman, it's difficult to be certain what his intentions were at that time. To give him the benefit of the doubt and assume that his motives were purely altruistic, consider the fact that Nixon was in power while the drug culture was in its infancy. It had not yet exploded into the deadly, widespread epidemic that plagues us today. Overdose deaths were relatively uncommon since the drugs were far less potent than they have become in recent years. Drug problems were also much more common among individuals who existed on the fringes of society. It would take several years for addiction to penetrate to the heart of mainstream America.

In 1970, Nixon signed the Controlled Substances Act into law.[53] This legislation classified drugs according to their use in medical applications and their propensity to be abused. Controlled substances were grouped on a five point scale according to schedule, with schedule 1 substances considered the most dangerous (least likely to be used for medical purposes and most likely to be abused). With Nixon's initial announcement of the war on drugs in 1971 came an increased budget for drug control agencies and new regulations that imposed mandatory sentences for drug offenders. He stated publicly that drugs were to be considered "public enemy number one." Although many criticized his tough on drugs policy as an unconstitutional overreach of big government, Nixon went on to win re-election in 1972. In 1973, he created the Drug Enforcement Agency (DEA) which received a budget of $75 million and 1,470 special agents.54 It was during this era and under this president that America's long and costly entanglement in this war against its own citizens was born. We end the discussion of Nixon's drug policies here as they were interrupted by his early resignation in 1974 at which time his role as president was relinquished to Gerald Ford.

Gerald Ford (Republican, 1974-1977)

In President Ford's first State of the Union Address in 1975, he called for mandatory minimum sentences for those convicted of involvement in the sale of "hard drugs," citing the legislation he had originally co-sponsored as a Congressman. HR 5946 called for a minimum of five years imprisonment for offenses involving transactions of four or more ounces of heroin and raised the minimum fine to $100,000 for organizations caught trafficking heroin into the U.S.55 It would be several more years, however, before these new sentencing guidelines would really start to increase the U.S. prison population.

During Ford's presidency, the number of imprisoned men in the United States was about one in 500—a number that had been relatively stable for five decades. As the war on drugs waged on, however, that number would double during the next decade, and quadruple during the decade after that.[56] Only about fifteen men per 100,000 were incarcerated for drug-related crimes in the 1970s, but that number would increase tenfold during the 20 year period that followed. [57]

Although Ford's drug policies were more or less an extension of Nixon's, he claimed to have engaged in negotiations with foreign leaders of countries (e.g. Columbia, Mexico, and Turkey) known to export drugs into the U.S. and asked them for assistance.[58] This would probably have been about as effective as politely asking an armed robber to put down his gun and walk away without your cash or your jewelry. But remember, most of our presidents have been much more interested in the *appearance* of fighting a war on drugs than they were committed to actually doing it. Meanwhile, the newly established drug culture in America was taking off over the pinball machines and under the flashy disco night club scene that characterized the 1970s.

Jimmy Carter (Democrat, 1977-1981)

It's no surprise that James Earl Carter, a Democrat who is now known for his compassion and humanitarian deeds, subscribed to an approach that was softer and more lenient than his two conservative predecessors. The one-term president was once quoted as saying, "Penalties for possession of a drug should not be more damaging to an individual than the use of the drug itself; and where they are, they should be changed."[59]

President Carter made it clear that he wasn't opposed to the legalization of marijuana, but did not actively pursue any policy changes on the issue while he was in office. The war on drugs faded into the background during the Carter years, as his administration did not significantly increase funding for drug enforcement, nor did he propose any legislation that would result in a marked change in the number of Americans in prison.

In 2011, on the fortieth anniversary of President Nixon's call for the war on drugs,, Carter wrote an op-ed that was published in *The New York Times* which stated that the war had failed in scope, purpose, and outcome, and should be terminated. He suggested a major paradigm shift in how we, as a nation, might better fix the deadly epidemic through improved methods of education, prevention, and treatment.[60]

Ronald Reagan (Republican, 1981-1989)

The Reagan years will always be remembered for First Lady, Nancy Reagan's "just say no" campaign which claimed to offer kids an uncomplicated way to escape peer pressure situations in which they might feel compelled to use drugs. Although undoubtedly pure in its intentions, "just say no" was heavily criticized as an impractical an overly simplistic idea that was clearly the brainchild of someone so far removed from any such scenario that few teenagers could relate. Nice try, Mrs. Reagan.

Incarceration of Americans, particularly drug offenders, skyrocketed during the Reagan years. In 1982, he reinstated the war on drugs originally called for by President Nixon that had lost momentum during the Carter presidency. Reagan made it clear that he viewed drugs more in terms of a direct threat to national security than a public health issue and offered little more than strict laws with stiff penalties as solutions. He signed the Anti-Drug Abuse Act of 1986 into law, which included longer mandatory minimum sentencing statutes that were triggered by lower quantities and expanded the existing policies to include marijuana and cocaine.[61] Another sweeping change included in this legislation was the provision that allowed courts to impose life sentences on second time drug offenders.[62] As the nation began to see arrests increase and more offenders being hit with long prison terms, some criticized the new laws, calling them draconian and insisting that they unfairly targeted blacks and other minorities. By the end of Reagan's second term, the percentage of men serving prison terms in the United States had doubled and was almost three times that of the average of the percentages of those in European nations.[63]

There was clearly some validity to the argument that Reagan's solution unfairly targeted black Americans through more stringent enforcement activity and the sentencing disparity that led to blacks receiving much longer prison terms for sales and possession of crack cocaine, which was more popular among blacks than the powder form of cocaine that was more frequently used by whites. Although both are the same drug, the sentencing guidelines that differed by a factor of ten to one remained unchallenged for years. Of course, it was mostly black Americans who paid the price. This also contributed to increases in violent crimes and gave rise to a host of social problems imposed on an already disadvantaged segment of the population. Keep in mind that while this is appalling to us, to the elites, who are strongly in favor of anything that leads to chaos, unrest, and instability in America, it was not only acceptable but celebrated.

As the incarceration rates soared to new heights under President Reagan, so did the public hysteria about addiction and drug-related crime, particularly regarding crack cocaine,64 Meanwhile drugs like MDMA (ecstasy) and methamphetamine were also gaining popularity. Despite the massive expansion of federal funds, manpower, and criminal prosecution of drug offenders that occurred during the 1980s, the rate of addiction remained relatively stable.65 In other words, it appears that the Reagan administration's efforts had little, if any, deterrent effect on the public. To be fair, it's possible that his actions and those of Congress might have slowed the progression and delayed it from rising to the level of a national crisis.

Although there is little evidence that proves Reagan was directly involved in the Iran-contra scandal, it did involve some key members of his administration who were not only accused of illegal arms trafficking and money laundering scandals but were also said to have allowed $4-5 billion worth of cocaine to be smuggled into and distributed within the United States. However, there is much more proof of involvement of CIA officials and Reagan's Vice President and successor, George H. W. Bush.[66]

Reagan had all the ideas and skills he needed to be a great president. His outsider status, campaign promises, and pre-election rhetoric had many voters hopeful that he would defeat the globalists' agenda. For example, he promised to dismantle the U.S. Department of Education and the Environmental Protection Agency, as he saw both as unnecessary, corrupt tools of the establishment with goals that served to benefit the elites at the expense of the American people. Two months into his first term, however, a nearly successful attempt on his life landed him on the operating table at George Washington University Medical Center. After that, his rhetoric was dramatically toned down and his softened policies suggested that he was intimidated into dancing to the establishment's drum. Note that the

Dept. of Ed. and EPA were never abolished and are both still very much alive and well today. Both receive more funding than ever before.

Who would have been Reagan's successor if the assassination attempt had succeeded? None other than the portrait of elitism, the world government puppet master's dream come true, and lifelong member of the Order of Skull and Bones, George Herbert Walker Bush. Of course, there are those who still believe he was shot because his actions offended a homicidal sociopath who was obsessed with Jodie Foster, but most of us now understand much more today than we did in 1981.

George H. W. Bush (Republican, 1989-1993)

Despite the fact that he posed as a conservative and a patriot, there is no question that George H.W. Bush was one of the most corrupt Presidents in American history. The entire Bush family personifies the very essence of elitism while their connections to notorious individuals and corrupt business practices are unparalleled in our history. America was the unfortunate victim of not one, but two Bush presidencies. The administration of George Bush Senior, former Vice President and Director of the CIA, was so tainted that Americans only trusted him to serve one term. His response to the growing drug epidemic was no more effective than the series of foreign policy blunders (e.g., the first invasion of Iraq) or broken campaign promises ("Read my lips, no new taxes") that will always be part of his legacy. His rhetoric and enormous allocation of federal funds to the drug epidemic would have been enough to make the average American believe he was passionately committed to eradicating drugs from our society, but as a sitting member of the Committee of 300 and the notorious Order of Skull and Bones secret society, he proved that his lifelong efforts were not intended to improve the lives of the American people, but to further the aims of elite globalists.

In his first State of the Union Address, Bush candidly called for a "new world order," which slipped by most Americans who weren't yet familiar with this term and had no idea what it meant.[67] Many will also remember the scripted, televised speech he delivered from the oval office in which he held up a bag containing what he claimed to be an ounce of crack cocaine seized by federal agents in a Washington, D.C. park located directly across from the White House. "It looks as innocent as candy, but it's turning out cities into battle zones," he said[68] Bush spoke of the urgency of the drug problem and outlined his administration's plan to escalate the war on drugs to a new level. When he took office in 1989 the budget for federal drug control agencies was $5 billion. When he left in 1993, it had been increased to $12 billion, the largest increase in history.[69] His approach was to severely punish everyone involved in the drug trade from traffickers and kingpins to the street dealers and users. His answer to a reporter who asked him how he proposed to solve the drug problem was simply, "more prisons, more jails, more courts, and more prosecutors."[70] He provided all of these which essentially locked the nation into the punitive system we live in today. He also militarized domestic forces such that 40,000 Americans had been the subjects of paramilitary style raids on their homes by federal drug enforcement agencies by the time he left office.[71]

George H, W. Bush added another component to the alleged effort to combat the drug problem by making it a foreign policy issue. Claiming to target international cartels (e.g., Honduras, El Salvador, Afghanistan, and others) he poured massive funding into weaponizing international anti-drug forces.[72] So who benefited most from all of this? Arms manufacturers, aerospace companies who supplied the helicopters, the growing military-industrial complex, and elite-owned multinational corporations. The elites have always been the financial benefactors of war. President Bush saw to it that the war on drugs was no exception.

In his 2010 book, *Shadow Masters*, Dr. Daniel Estulin discusses George H. W. Bush's long history of abusing the power he held in high-level federal positions to facilitate illegal arms trading, human rights violations, and the many crimes of international drug cartels:

> "The CIA did not just deal drugs during the Iran-Contra era; it has done so for the full fifty years of its history. Today I will give you evidence which will show that the CIA, and many figures who became known during Iran-Contra such as Richard Secord, Ted Shackley, Tom Clines, Felix Rodriguez and George Herbert Walker Bush, have been selling drugs to Americans since the Vietnam era."[73]

As he left office, President Bush confirmed his corruption when he pardoned six Reagan-era officials who were charged with federal crimes connected to the Iran-contra scandal,[74] leaving an indelible stain on American institutions for which many have never re-gained any trust.

To summarize Bush's accomplishments in terms of the war on drugs, they included harsh legislation that targeted and punished Americans, massive funding that weaponized and militarized domestic and foreign anti-drug forces, the further enrichment of special interests and defense contractors, and further empowerment of ruthless, barbaric drug lords and cartels. His policies, however, had no effect whatsoever on reducing the number of Americans using drugs,[75] despite the record number of offenders who were imprisoned under his watch, many of whom remain in custody to this day. Anyone who wanted to see America solve its crippling drug problem would view George H. W. Bush as a monumental failure. His loyalty to the elites, however, undoubtedly made him quite a hero in their eyes.

Bill Clinton (Democrat, 1993-2001)

Although the Clinton presidency is remembered by many as a golden era of peace and prosperity, we now know that the Clinton administration was corrupt to its core. Prior to being selected for the presidency, William Jefferson Clinton is said to have been a key player in assisting the importation of massive quantities of cocaine into the U.S. and the exportation of arms to the Nicaraguan Contras through the small airport in Mena, Arkansas while he served as Governor.76

On policy, one of the most sweeping and memorable accomplishments of the Clinton Administration was the notorious 1994 Crime Bill, which essentially led to even more mass incarceration, particularly of black males. The lopsided sentencing disparity between rock and crack cocaine was noted by the advisory board Clinton tasked with investigating it, although he ultimately ignored their findings and signed the bill anyway despite urgent warnings from those closest to him about the implications it would have on people of color. His public stance on illegal drug use among average citizens was rigid and unforgiving, while he was noticeably soft with regard to holding top bankers and more prominent figures in the drug trade accountable for similar crimes.

A 2016 article in *The Guardian* stated the following about Clinton: "The former president made sure low-level drug users felt the full weight of state power at the same moment bankers saw the shackles that bound them removed."77 Although many remember Bill Clinton as the president who "didn't inhale," as he insisted when grilled by reporters inquiring about whether he smoked marijuana in college, there is ample evidence to suggest that he did much more than that. When his brother, Roger Clinton, was arrested for possession of cocaine, he was videotaped saying, "I need to get some for my brother. He's got a nose like a Hoover vacuum cleaner." There are also multiple residents of Arkansas who have signed sworn affidavits detailing their experiences using drugs with Bill and Hillary Clinton, as well as reports from several Arkansas State Police officers who served as Clinton's bodyguards while he was governor that confirmed the former President's heavy use of cocaine.

So why did Bill Clinton appear to have such a tough stance against illicit drugs? The answer is quite simple. Walter Mondale's stunning defeat by Ronald Reagan in 1984, and that of Michael Dukakis to George H.W. Bush in 1988 had left the Democrat Party scrambling to re-define itself. In their discussions, a plan to distance themselves from blacks and other minority groups and project an image that would appeal to white voters and wealthy corporate donors who had been lost to failed liberal policies was agreed upon. A "no-nonsense" position on crime, which called for 100,000 additional police officers on the streets and even tougher mandatory minimum sentences were elements of the proposed path to victory for Clinton—a strategy that clearly succeeded given the substantial margin of his victory over the incumbent President Bush in 1992.[78]

The billions of dollars' worth of cocaine that Clinton and his acolytes helped to traffic into the United States suggest that he had no personal ambitions aligned with keeping dangerous and addictive drugs off of our streets, out of our schools, or away from our communities. His willingness to enact legislation that would effectively banish tens of thousands of black men to the prison system was done simply because it was politically advantageous for him at the time. In 2011, however, Clinton made a public statement joining former President Carter in his call for an end to the war on drugs.[79]

George W. Bush (Republican, 2001-2009)

One of the only periods in the history of the war on drugs that actually saw a slight decline in overall illicit drug use among young people was during the two-term presidency of George W. Bush. His administration's strategy had three key elements, which he described as a "balanced approach:" preventing drug use before it starts, intervening and healing those who already use drugs, and disrupting the market for illicit substances. "Bush W.," as he was often called to distinguish him from his father, began by starting the first ever National Drug Control Strategy (NDCS).[80] Despite the corruption and scandal that many associate with the Bush dynasty, and although much of their energy while they were in power was spent catering to the globalists' (e.g., the "Patriot Act" which used the threat of terrorism as leverage to justify suspending the civil liberties of American citizens), it appears that this president's actions may have actually led to some positive results. Perhaps his own personal history of alcohol and cocaine use gave him a glimpse of life from the addict's perspective.

Although President Bush did not attempt to repeal any of the strict laws that were established by his predecessors, his approach added significant resources for treatment and prevention. He proposed a $1 billion funding grant for treatment programs which was to be distributed among the fifty states, with follow-up studies to assess each state's specific need.[81] At the time he was in office, drug use was predominantly an urban problem. Seeing this, Bush launched the Major Cities Initiative which targeted twenty-five metropolitan areas with education and prevention campaigns. Of course, during Bush's eight years in office, the drugs that were most problematic were marijuana, cocaine, methamphetamine, heroin, and MDMA, so these drugs were the targets of his efforts. The enormous problem we face today with prescription opiates was only beginning to take shape in the early 2000s.

At the end of Bush's presidency, he submitted a detailed progress report to Congress, praising his administration's accomplishments. It stated that overall drug use among eighth, tenth, and twelfth grade students in the U.S. had decreased by 19 percent during his two terms.[82] The report identified the factors he believed had been most responsible for the positive results (e.g., Partnership for a Drug-Free America, et. al.) and offered suggestions for how to keep the country on a positive trajectory. Of course, a new wave of deadly drugs was about to take a firm grip on the populace, and the administration that took power when Bush left office would unravel most of the progress that had been made.

The fact that some moderate improvements in the nation's drug problem took place while George W. Bush was in office should not be seen as evidence that he or the Bush family weren't guiding the nation, full speed ahead, toward world government. His actions did not cease to enrich the military-industrial complex, nor will they ever negate the costly and unethical war in Iraq, U.S. occupation in

Afghanistan, or suspicions surrounding the September 11th, 2001 terror attack that killed more than 3,000 innocent Americans. Questions about whether Bush administration officials were directly involved, had prior knowledge, ordered U.S. forces to "stand-down," and/or participated in a cover-up still remain unanswered. While there may have been fewer young Americans using drugs when Bush left office, the overall state of the nation, particularly the failing economy, was worse by practically every metric. Things would get a lot worse before they would get better.

Let's be clear. The Bush administration's limited success on drug policy was temporary and did nothing to prepare us for the tidal wave of addiction that was forthcoming. While a few tally marks might have been made in the column of victories for America while the Bushes were at the helm, those wins are inconsequential when viewed alongside the losses that more than cancel them out. Overall, the elites got richer and the corporatocracy gained power while the American people suffered economic hardship and the further erosion of our freedoms.

During no period in American history was there an increase in drug addiction rates on the scale of that which occurred during the Obama Administration. An increase of several hundred percentage points in overdose deaths by prescription opiates occurred between 2008 and 2016.[83] More than 249 million prescriptions for opiates were written nationwide between November 2015 and November 2016, which is nearly one per every US citizen.[84] This figure, of course, does not take into account prescription drugs that were sold on the black market and therefore represents a conservative approximation of opiates that were consumed by Americans during that period.

Throughout Obama's two term presidency he was careful to avoid using the term "war on drugs" in his speeches. His rhetoric demonstrated his view that the nation's drug problem should be approached as a public health matter rather than a criminal justice issue. It's unclear exactly how much his actions might have been motivated by his own personal history, as he openly admitted to using marijuana and cocaine as a teenager and young adult. One of his campaign promises stated that his administration would tackle criminal justice reform, although he was unable to get Congress on board with a comprehensive bill that would shift the government's focus away from attacking the suppliers of drugs (aggressively prosecuting dealers, cartels, and smugglers) and addressing those who create the demand (education, prevention, and treatment). So he took matters into his own hands by urging prisoners who were serving long sentences for non-violent drug crimes to petition for early release. Out of over 36,000 applicants only about 18,000 were denied. Nearly half were approved which resulted in a significant reduction in the federal prison population for the first time in three decades. It should be noted, however, that he did not take any significant steps in this direction during his first term. In fact, he didn't start releasing federal inmates until the end of 2016, just weeks before he left office.[85]

In 2013, the Obama administration instructed the Department of Justice to move forward with the "Smart on Crime Initiative,"[86] which included no official legislative change to repeal any draconian statutes that were on the books at that time. It was more of an informal request sent to prosecutors throughout the nation asking them to stop trying cases that would result in the incarceration of offenders. The federal prison population dropped from approximately 209,000 inmates who were incarcerated when he took office in 2009 to fewer than 190,000 at the end of his second term.87 Although his approach to the nation's drug problem was ideologically antithetical to traditional strategies, and more in line with what the "experts" and drug legalizers had been calling for, the epidemic continued to grow and claim record numbers of lives during every year of Obama's command. This is not surprising considering that his entire first term was spent simply looking the other way, and his second term, undermining the hard work that hundreds of prosecutors had put forth convicting these offenders, and releasing thousands of potentially dangerous criminals into America's communities.

Afghanistan's rate of opium production reportedly increased by 43 percent during the period between 2015 and 2016, with more than 4,800 tons of heroin pouring into world markets in Europe, Russia, and the United States.88 Obama's policies greatly contributed to the crisis in America as he thwarted investigations into Afghanistan's drug trafficking, and refused to prosecute criminal cases presented to the Department of Justice that involved the trafficking of pharmaceutical grade opioids. His soft policies at the

US/Mexico border also contributed to untold amounts of heroin and other dangerous narcotics freely flowing in as border patrol agents were routinely ordered to "stand down."[89]

It is now suspected that Barack Obama's policies were influenced by his puppet master and personal slush fund, globalist billionaire George Soros, who has been called "the world's biggest drug legalizer." Soros is, of course, a long standing member of the Committee of 300 who is also beholden to the British crown, the original progenitors of a similar opiate war waged against China decades ago.[90] In addition to his failed enforcement policies, Obama also sabotaged the US healthcare system, thereby ensuring that those Americans who found themselves addicted to opiate drugs would no longer have the benefits necessary to seek treatment or recovery.

Although Obama often spoke of the need to address the nation's growing drug epidemic, his actions suggest that he had no such intentions as he left office without ever making any significant progress toward a solution. He made enormous strides, however, in terms of furthering the global elites' agenda, having left the nation significantly more divided, addicted, and dependent than he found it, and perhaps more so than it had been at any point since the Civil War.

Donald Trump (Republican, 2017-Present)

President Trump has done more in three years to combat the opiate crisis than Barack Obama did during his two full terms as president. He has called on Congress to provide legislation that will curb the opiate crisis by one-third over the next three years.[91] In 2017, he declared the epidemic a public health emergency which activated the deployment of assistance programs and redirected funding for research and development strategies and programs aimed at treatment and prevention.[92] He has called for harsh penalties for opium traffickers, suggesting that they face the death penalty and that selling lower quantities of opiates should trigger mandatory sentences for dealers.[93]

Unlike his predecessor, Trump fulfilled his campaign promise to accomplish criminal justice reform, which gave a large number of non-violent offenders who had been model prisoners and demonstrated a desire to succeed, a second chance. Trump also donated his entire third-quarter salary (approximately $125,000) from 2017 to the Department of Health and Human Services, earmarking the contribution for use in the federal government's response to the opiate crisis.94

Donald Trump is different from all other presidents in modern history. He was not chosen by the elites, nor are his actions beholden to them. In fact, he's turned the decades-old paradigm inside Washington's political circles on its head. Not only did the elites not choose Trump as a political candidate, they vehemently opposed him and piled on top of one another to throw everything they had at trying to stop him. They have continued to launch brutal attacks against him daily, up to and including the theatrical impeachment proceedings we were forced to endure as we rang in the new decade.

Despite the controversy that has surrounded Trump since the early days of his campaign, Americans seem likely to re-elect him in November 2020. And why wouldn't we? He's on a dedicated mission to repair decades of damage done by anti-American globalists who have hijacked top level positions within our government to ensure our demise while serving their own selfish interests. While some presidents accomplish less during their second (lame duck) terms, we can expect the opposite from Donald Trump. If you believe he's rogue and unhinged now, strap in! His second term is sure to be unrestrained as he continues to put America first!

We finally have a president who truly cares about the future of America and the lives of our young people. He's committed to ending the senseless loss of life caused by this epidemic. The mainstream media outlets, however, firmly rooted in their perpetual quest to control your worldview, downplay these facts. His disruption of the traditional "business as usual" mantra in Washington is precisely the reason why he's the subject of endless ridicule from the press and career politicians, and was the catalyst for the failed attempt to remove him from office—a colossal waste of time and resources that embarrassed the nation and set reckless and dangerous precedent for all future leaders.

Trump himself is a tee-totaller as he has been his entire life. This came at the insistence of his late brother, Fred, who died at the age of forty-three from alcoholism. Donald adored his brother, who died leaving a permanent soft spot on his heart for those who struggle with substance abuse issues.95 He was vigilant in his insistence that his own children grow up sober, as his daughter Ivanka recalled in a 2016 interview, "Every day before we went to school, he told us, 'No alcohol. No drugs. No cigarettes.'"[96] First Lady, Melania Trump, has also shown a sincere interest in bringing public awareness to the drug epidemic by visiting addiction clinics in America's heartland, holding opiate-addicted babies in her arms and speaking to recovering addicts with words intended to empower and encourage them through their difficult journeys.[97]

There is some evidence that Trump's policies are making a difference in the national crisis, even though we need to do so much more. In his 2020 State of the Union Address, the president stated:

> "With unyielding commitment, we are curbing the opiate epidemic. Last year I reported that drug overdose deaths declined for the first time in nearly thirty years. Among the states hardest hit, Ohio is down 22 percent, Pennsylvania is down 18 percent, Wisconsin is down 10 percent, and we will not quit until we have beaten this epidemic once and for all."[98]

Trump's historic tax cuts, slashing of burdensome regulations, and hard line efforts to secure the southern border are all indicators that he is not a puppet for the globalists. Although the wealth and influence behind him have resulted in numerous attempts to recruit him into elite secret societies, he has consistently declined. His worldview and view of the nation are in direct conflict with the aspiring world government. He based his entire campaign on American nationalism and fighting the forces that have been gutting the United States for generations. He loves America. Pure and simple. Why else would he trade the comfortable retirement he could have enjoyed with the fruits of his labor earned in the course of a successful career in business for a stressful, demanding, tumultuous, political fight that has caused him to be the subject of endless threats, criticism, and vitriol? My 2017 book, *For the Love of Trump: The Historic 2016 Presidential Election from the Perspective of a Social Media Warrior*, discusses Trump's long history of kind, generous acts, his patriotism, and the reasons behind his bid for the presidency. He's one of us, and we must give him four more years to continue working tirelessly (and for free) on our behalf.

It's been said many times that the war on drugs is actually a war on us. No one can deny the social woes it has created in and of itself—some that are arguably more detrimental than those caused by the use of drugs in the first place.

Again, since the war on drugs was declared nearly five decades ago the number of Americans incarcerated for minor drug offenses has multiplied. The U.S. accounts for 5 percent of the world population but houses 25 percent of the world prison population, the vast majority of those serving time for non-violent drug offenses.[99]

The number of homicides in the U.S. has also increased exponentially over the last 50 years—a fact that can be attributed to the lack of access drug dealers have to the court system which leaves them no alternatives to violence to settle their disputes.[100] The fear of legal consequences has also factored into overdose deaths, as people tend to ingest illegal substances out of public view, so there's no one around to help if and when problems arise. Another very common scenario that leads to overdose deaths plays out as follows: when people are released from jail custody or rehabilitation programs, their tolerance for drugs has been reduced to a fraction of what it had been during periods of heavy use. In fact, with enough time, tolerance can return to the level of a first-time user, so taking a dose equivalent to what one may have tolerated previously has a greater potential to be fatal. Do all of these facts add up to suggest that we're going about this all wrong?

Keep in mind that the term "war on drugs" is euphemistic rhetoric created only to convince us that our government is pulling out all the stops to try to solve this problem. It was never meant to succeed. It has failed to meet its stated objectives *by design*. Look at the devastating statistics, then consider the size and strength of our massive and powerful government which, in spite of its vast economic resources, has conveniently stood by, stood down, and pretended to watch helplessly as this nightmare of addiction, which will claim the lives of millions of American victims before it's over, has unfolded.

Considering how the elites have dictated many of our policies and created the drug culture in the first place, is it any wonder their so-called efforts to remedy the problem have proven to be unsuccessful? These failures are not the result of incompetence, ineptitude, or ignorance of the facts. Rather, it's clear that those responsible know exactly what they're doing. There's too much evidence contrary to the idea that efforts to solve this national dilemma have failed due to negligence or lack of qualified leadership. Who are the winners and losers in this war? The military-industrial complex has been enriched as have other corrupt forces throughout the world. Meanwhile, the government's reach into our lives has been strengthened as our civil rights have been further subverted.

There's no question that they've exerted enormous influence over us through music, TV, and Hollywood. We know that their half-hearted solutions have exacerbated the problems. We also know that they've taken control of the education system to promote the drug culture and disrupt each child's ability to think for him or herself. The next chapter discusses a century of attacks waged against America's children by way of the public schools.

CHAPTER 4

**Wolves in Sheep's Clothing:
Drug Education in U.S. Schools**

The most extensively documented mind control attacks waged against Americans involve the hijacking of the education system. The elites have a history of controlling what our children are learning in school that dates back over a hundred years. Fortunately, their efforts to change the fundamental goals of education have been exposed by whistleblower and national treasure, Charlotte Thomson Iserbyt, who discovered their underhanded scheme while holding a top-level position in the U.S. Department of Education under President Reagan.

In 1999, Iserbyt published her groundbreaking book, *The Deliberate Dumbing Down of America: A Chronological Paper Trail,* which provides compelling evidence that the non-profit organizations including the Ford and Rockefeller Foundations and the Carnegie Corporation have been funding curriculum changes that brainwash American children to align with Communist/Marxist ideology since the early part of the 20th century.[101] Their goals? To shift the focus of education from traditional academics to outcome-based competence and program children to embrace collectivism over individualism, to destroy the conscience, and to prepare each child for a lifetime of servitude within a planned, socialist economic system of world government.

As a young woman, Iserbyt held positions in the U.S. State Department and traveled overseas where she was exposed to the horrors of Communism. After completing her assignments abroad, she returned to the United States and enrolled her children in the public school system in Camden, Maine. It didn't take long for her to realize that the most fundamental principles of American education were being challenged and changed dramatically. Although voicing opposition to the changes made her very unpopular, she had no idea who was behind all of it or why it was being done. Getting the answers to these questions set her on a course of activism that would continue for forty years.

Deeply concerned about some of the propaganda her sons brought home from school, Iserbyt secured a position on the local school board. She created a grassroots, conservative organization called "Guardians of Education for Maine," which successfully blocked some of the curriculum changes that were proposed in her state. She learned of an elaborate, concerted effort that was underway to subvert the national goals of education one school at a time by way of specially trained "change agents." The instructions came from a handbook titled *Innovations in Education: A Change Agent's Guide*.102 Agents were trained to con parents and influential people in the community into supporting the implementation of programs like Drug and Alcohol Ed., Sex Ed., Death Ed., etc. Their job was to convince the public that these programs were necessary to prevent students from experimenting with drugs and alcohol, engaging in premature sexual encounters, or attempting suicide.

At the time these programs were being pushed, drug use and promiscuity among teens was virtually unheard of, especially in the smaller towns and rural areas. It was a combination of these targeted "education" campaigns and the newly created drug culture invented and injected into society by the Tavistock Institute that actually caused illicit drug use in American schools to surface. Iserbyt would go on to discover that this had been their intention all along.

Change agents were taught how to identify and overcome those who would resist curriculum changes by singling them out and ostracizing them. Iserbyt found all of this to be extremely bizarre, as she was being taught to identify herself. She was roundly criticized for her belief that education should stay focused on academics and instilling traditional values that would mold students into good citizens. Eventually she learned that directives from the top levels of the education system were actually intended to destroy the values students had been taught at home, blur their senses of right and wrong, and ensure that they were prepared for a lifetime of compliant subservience in the new world the elites had been planning for many years.

Obviously she found all of this to be very troubling, but it wasn't until she got recruited to work in the U.S. Department of Education's Office of Research and Improvement that the pieces of this complex puzzle would start to come together. Her position gave her access to thousands of pages of documents that had been left by previous administrators. The more she read, the more it became clear to her that there was a dark and deeply sinister conspiracy to destroy the United States and the American capitalist system using Skinnerian/Pavlovian conditioning techniques in the schools to make children incapable of independent thought or self-determination.

Iserbyt was ultimately terminated from her job at the Department of Ed. as she was unable to ignore the evil of this plot. When a memo came across her desk from "Better Education Skills through Technology, or B.E.S.T., she learned of the proposed plan to use powerful computer software programs to brainwash the children and was understandably horrified. At the top of the memo appeared the words. "what we are able to control and manipulate at the local level." She could no longer remain silent and leaked this document to the press. Although this action got her fired, the information did not receive the community attention it deserved, so Iserbyt voiced her concerns in a detailed letter to President Reagan which explained the insidious corruption that was going on in the department. Receiving no official response to her letter and being a rather tenacious and civic-minded member of America's best generation, she published *The Deliberate Dumbing Down of America*, which has been translated to multiple languages and distributed around the world.

Charlotte Iserbyt's extensive writing includes very little about drugs being used as a tool to destroy young minds and weaken the United States as a nation. The evil she exposes, however, and with meticulous fact-referencing, goes to the very core of the globalists' agenda. It speaks to the depths they are willing to sink to in their quest for world domination. By providing direct quotes and in many cases the original source documents, she makes an airtight case that proves beyond a doubt that the tax-exempt foundations were the architects of a blueprint to "dumb down" America's children since the early 1900s. The light she has shed on their commitment to the end goal of destroying the futures of millions of innocent children by poisoning their minds makes it clear that there is little we can put past them. Suddenly, the accusations of evil that others have assigned to them become not only possible, but likely.

Throughout the twentieth century, the education system in America was gradually and ever so quietly re-engineered as huge endowments from the elites were traded for influence.[103] The change agents manipulated parents and teachers at the grassroots level and standardized curriculum and assessment tests to ensure that every child was tailored to their desired specifications. Those who were not would be identified and held back until the target outcome was demonstrated. By exposing us to outcome-based education and values clarification all day at school and the malicious

Tavistock Institute drug culture propaganda we came home to on our televisions and radios at night, the elites were able to harness enormous control over our developing minds. To varying degrees, they limited many of our futures, dampened our dreams, and corrupted our minds—and they did it all without shame and with absolute impunity.

The drug education curriculum developed and forced through the schools during the 1970s, 80s, and 90s was predominantly fear-driven (e.g., "this is your brain on drugs") propaganda that decreed abstinence and threatened non-compliance with a host of moral, health, and legal consequences. But much of the instruction was presented in language that piqued curiosity and sparked a desire in many students to experiment, particularly those predisposed to rebellion. Consider the following passage extracted from an 8th grade Health class textbook from 1982: "immediately after [the drug is] ingested, the user experiences a pleasurable, euphoric sense of well-being that may last for up to 30 minutes." Another states, "the user enters a dreamlike state during which wild hallucinations of bright colors and vivid images from deep within the imagination might be experienced."[104]

The same textbook includes two pages of full-color photos of pipes, hypodermic syringes, powdered cocaine, LSD blots, caffeine, amphetamine capsules, benzodiazepine pills, and small, multi-colored balloons filled with heroin and other drugs to demonstrate how they are often smuggled inside the human body to avoid detection. Opposite the photos is a table listing each class of drugs with lists of their corresponding street names ("Mary Jane," "yellow jackets," "snow white," "horse," and "sweet dreams").[105] Is it even necessary to explain how these instructional materials planted seeds of curiosity in impressionable young minds? Without objection, we move on.

Programs like D.A.R.E. made their debut in the late 1980s. Most follow-up studies that were carried out to gauge their effectiveness as deterrents for future drug use among teens found no significant benefits. Such programs, although perhaps well-intended and not without merit, were criticized as over-simplistic and for lacking a connection to students' real life experiences. If these programs had any positive influence on a child's future decision about using drugs, the effects did not stand the test of time.[106] Of course, we can only evaluate these programs by operating under the assumption that their goal was to actually prevent or delay students from drug use. Sadly, we're unable to proceed with that as a given since the elites, in many cases, initiated these programs fully expecting them to accomplish exactly the opposite.

We have lost the ability to make choices about the curriculum taught in American schools. In 2018, the state of California became the first to require "LGBT sensitivity" training for elementary school children. These children are quite arguably too young to learn about sexuality in any capacity, let alone sex between same-gender partners. Participation in these courses is mandatory in that parents are not allowed to opt their children out of it.107

While parents across the U.S. were busy fighting "Common Core" on the national level, the Trojan horse was being ushered in quietly in the name of charter schools and school choice. The term "school choice," sounds like a great policy, right? Who wouldn't be in favor of having a choice about which school your child attends? But few Americans see school choice for what it really is, another clever attempt to deceive us. The average person fails to understand that the proposals for charter schools and the school choice program take control from elected school boards that gave parents and concerned citizens a voice and place it in the hands of unelected bureaucrats.[108] With unelected boards, you have no one to go to if you have a problem or a complaint. Re-structuring is modeled after the Communist Soviet system and ultimately threatens to undermine our entire representative form of government.

The fight to take back control of American schools is literally a battle between good and evil—a battle for the hearts and minds of every child who will be affected by the outcome. We must get intimately involved in what our children are being taught in school and speak out against the changes that have transformed our schools into socialist indoctrination centers that systematically destroy a child's conscience while introducing them to what those at the top hope will be lifelong drug habits. This is discussed in more detail in Chapter 9.

CHAPTER 5

The Powerful and Corrupt: Governments Aligned with Cartels and the International Drug Trade

What I'm about to describe is graphic and certainly not intended for the weak at heart. About a year ago, a friend showed me a horrific video. The unspeakable cruelty and callous disregard for human life it depicted left me stunned. The heart-wrenching sounds and images will stay with me forever. The video opened to a scene that showed four masked men with machine guns in a wooded area. They stood above a Hispanic male who appeared to be in his late thirties or early forties. He was next to a teenage boy (presumably his son) and both of them were on their knees. One of the men was angrily yelling at them in Spanish. Suddenly, he handed his machine gun off to one of the others and pulled out a large knife. He grabbed the man by his hair to violently jerk him closer.

Still holding him by the hair, he put the knife against the man's throat and started sawing. Bright red blood gushed from his neck and splattered onto the ground in front of him. He did not resist as the slicing back and forth continued, although he struggled to breathe after his windpipe was severed. The boy whimpered as he watched from a few feet away. He continued to hack at the man's neck until his head was completely detached and his lifeless body fell limp onto the ground, his head still hanging from his hair in the hand of his brutal attacker. He tossed the man's head into the bushes about 20 feet away, the masked men all laughing as it rolled along the ground making a thumping sound when it hit the trunk of a tree.

It gets much worse. He grabbed the boy and forced him to his feet, making him stand straight with his back against a tree. Using the same knife, he stabbed the boy's chest then moved the knife sideways making a large gash in his skin. The boy tried to be brave and made almost no sounds as the barbaric killer ripped the skin from his chest, using his bare hands, applying the knife to slice through the tougher parts of his torso until his ribs and lungs were fully exposed. He reached into the boy's chest and pulled out his pounding heart. With a single slice he cut the vessels that it was attached to. The boy was still fighting to breathe as the man shoved his heart back into his chest, stabbed him a few more times and dropped his lifeless body next to the headless corpse on the ground. He used the last bit of life force he had left to reach out and try to pull himself closer to his father. The armed men laugh, and the scene closes. The End.

Needless to say, I was appalled and horrified as my mind flooded with so many questions that I wasn't even sure which one to ask first. Who were these people? Where did this happen? And what had this father and son done to deserve this gruesome, tortuous execution? Why had someone recorded this savage butchery and posted it on the internet for all to see? I asked these questions once I got past the speechlessness brought on by the horrific, raw debauchery I had just witnessed.

It was explained to me why the events in this video took place and why it was just one of hundreds of similar videos that are easily accessible by performing a simple Google search. It had been filmed earlier that year in a state in Northern Mexico just a few miles south of the U.S./Mexico border. It was created and posted by the "Zetas," one of the largest and most notorious cartels operating in the world today. Much has been written about them and their activities during the last few years. What had the man and his son done to meet with such a horrific and agonizing fate?

I was sickened to learn that they were killed simply for trespassing. They were crossing over land that's controlled exclusively by the Zetas because it's part of a route used to smuggle cocaine, heroin, and methamphetamine into the U.S. It's strictly forbidden to everyone else, so anyone caught there without express permission is deemed a threat to the operation, which is punishable by death. Some trespassers are shot. Some are hanged. Others have limbs sawed off or are decapitated. It's up to their captors to decide, and in cases where excessive brutality is used, the killings are often videotaped and posted to the internet to send a clear message, "Enter our land and this is what will happen to you!"

Judging from the number of videos available depicting these heinous killings and dozens of news reports of beheaded and dismembered bodies found in these areas, these merciless acts of human depravity are simply "business as usual" for organized criminals who are willing to obliterate anything or anyone that stands in their way, and they want everyone to know it. They're heavily armed and, in many cases, trained in tactical and guerilla warfare and paramilitary operations. They're vile, heartless killers. By definition, they're terrorists!

I apologize for taking your through the vivid details of this video, but felt it was the best way, perhaps the only way, to illustrate the unyielding power and heartlessness that fuels the international drug trade. In his 2014 Book, *Shadow Masters*, Daniel Estulin describes drug sales as the "lubricant for the global economy," with approximately $930,000,000,000 changing hands every year.[109] Other sources suggest that this is a conservative estimate as most of the money involved in drug transactions is never officially reported by any country, which makes the exact amount impossible to quantify.

Corrupt leaders who conduct secret business deals have been put into positions of power all over the world in nations that don't have democratic elections. Cartel money is used to rig elections and promote candidates who cater to drug traffickers in nations that do. For decades, dirty drug money has been used to set the global stage that allows the international drug trade to flourish. In areas where their operatives have not been able to infiltrate the local political system that blocks them from their markets, they don't hesitate to use violence and intimidation to further their objectives.

The determination of those who profit from drugs smuggled into the U.S. from Mexico was put on display in the border town of Laredo Nuevo in 2005. Fifty-eight year old father of three, Alejandro Dominguez Coello was sworn in as the city's new police chief following a string of murders that had left the acting chief and five other local officers dead. At his swearing in, Coelllo told reporters that he had "no fear," and spoke of his commitment to apprehending drug traffickers and running the cartels out of town. Less than six hours later, he was ambushed by gunfire and killed in broad daylight as he was climbing into his truck.[110] More than fifty shell casings were found at the scene of his murder which was clearly intended to send a message about what could happen to anyone who might be thinking about interfering with the cartel's mission.

American intelligence forces and the Mexican government have identified the Guzman-Sinaloa cartel as the most powerful In the world.[111] This is, of course, the organized crime ring that was led by the notorious El Chapo Guzman, who was apprehended in Guatemala and extradited to a maximum security Mexican prison. His elaborate escape in July of 2015 was facilitated by a team of men who were paid by the cartel to dig two miles of tunnel that ended under Guzman's prison cell. Although he was eventually captured and taken back into custody, his historic escape speaks to the sheer muscle and persistence behind these organized criminal enterprises.

The strongest cartels in the world today rose to power during the 1980s and 1990s. They're anything but rag-tag groups of amateur criminals. Although their objectives are criminal in nature, they're highly sophisticated and organized, employing chemists, financial advisors, assassins, and people from dozens of otherwise respectable professions who work toward their two primary goals: to control the market price of their product, and to eliminate any force that would compete with or block their market.[112]

In 2010, a total of 8,900 pounds of illicit drugs were seized by U.S. officials at the U.S./Mexico border. In 2018, more than 82,000 pounds were seized.[113] It's unclear exactly why the number has increased nearly ten-fold in an eight-year period. Could it be that the growing demand for drugs in the U.S. has called for more product to be trafficked (and therefore seized)? Is it because more traffickers have started bringing drugs directly into Mexico and using our southern border as the port of entry? Or could it be that seizures have increased because we finally have a president who has empowered border patrol agents through increased funding and policies that actually allow them to do their jobs? The answer is likely to be a combination of all of these factors.

In November 2019, President Donald Trump stated his intention to declare war on the Mexican drug cartels, which included labeling them as international terror organizations, an action that would have serious implications as it would prohibit U.S. citizens from engaging in any action that would benefit cartel interests. It would have also made it illegal for U.S. banks to engage in business transactions with them, and prohibit anyone associated with the cartels from entering the U.S. Trump's decision was a reaction to the horrific story of a small caravan of American citizens who were ambushed with gunfire as they traveled about 70 miles south of the U.S./Mexico border. Three women and six children were killed in cold blood as they plead for their lives in this attack that sparked outrage across the nation. [114]

In response to a request from Mexico's President Andrés Manuel López Obrador, President Trump agreed to temporarily delay branding the cartels as terrorist groups until leaders from both countries could engage in negotiations.115 Obrador's request is an indication of the extent to which Mexico's economy depends on the cartels and the revenue generated through the drug market in the United States. The cartels exercise enormous power within the corrupt government of Mexico, such that fear of retaliation probably also motivated Obrador to ask Trump to delay taking action that could disrupt their operations.

In the 1980s, the drug route for cocaine, which was produced primarily in Columbia, used airlines and ships to bring drugs through the Caribbean and into U.S. ports in Miami. In the 1990s, the U.S. Drug Enforcement Agency and U.S. Customs reportedly dedicated nearly one billion dollars in resources to shutting down this trade route through which drugs from several Central and South American countries were flowing. To continue moving their products into the U.S., they started sending shipments to Mexico and transporting them across ground—a seamless transition as local cartels were already experts at smuggling across our border. Assisting them with moving their products through

Mexico via land has proven to be extremely lucrative for the Mexican government.116 Should this route become blocked, rest assured that another pathway will be found, at least as long as the demand exists and markets in the U.S. continue to make these operations so profitable.

According to Dr. Daniel Estulin, without drug money the economic systems of entire nations would collapse on themselves.117 When we consider that close to a trillion dollars is moved around the world in drug trade every year, the motivation that drives endless violence, corruption, and secrecy becomes much easier to understand, as do the relationships that exist between government officials, cartel operatives, and elites who head multi-national corporations that circulate illegal drugs and "dirty" money through the system, all thereby further enriching themselves.

There is no question that drugs are exchanged for weapons that are used against individuals, communities and entire nations, although finding evidence of this can require one to do some digging. When the CIA and some of our high level elected officials were found to be involved in arms trading and illegal drug trafficking, most Americans reacted with shock and disbelief. Some were outraged while others felt deeply ashamed and profoundly disappointed that our "trusted" officials and government agencies participated in these scandals. The truth, however, is that the CIA has been deeply and continuously involved in international drug trafficking for decades.[118] And why wouldn't they be? After all, we've entrusted them with unlimited taxpayer funding and unfettered, unrestrained power. We demand no oversight or accountability, and simply accept their assertions that we must be kept in the dark to protect national security interests. Doesn't that sound like a situation that's rife for abuse and corruption?

Aren't we owed an explanation for how our money is spent, not to mention how our nation's reputation and standing in the world are affected by the activities that are carried out by our own institutions that supposedly represent our values? Should we blindly accept their claims that billions of dollars that are never accounted for are spent on poorly defined "covert operations?"

A fairly recent and well documented example of high-level corruption was dubbed the "Fast and Furious" scandal that took place during the Obama administration. When the CIA was accused of supplying arms to the Mexican Sinaloa cartel, they claimed it was necessary to assist them in their fight against the Zetas, a rival cartel that they feared was so powerful it could potentially overthrow the Mexican government and take over the entire nation of Mexico. Multiple whistleblowers from the CIA and DEA, however, exposed the fact that the CIA had also been shipping arms to the Zetas while providing some of their fighters with tactical training in paramilitary operations at a secret camp in Texas. In exchange, the CIA was allowing untold quantities of deadly, illegal drugs to be imported into the United States. Some of the weapons provided to the cartels were later used to kill U.S. Border Patrol agents and law enforcement personnel.[119]

All of this allegedly took place with full knowledge of top officials in the Justice Department and the Obama administration.[120] To this day, however, no one has been held accountable. No one has even been pressed for an official explanation. But what more could we expect from organizations to which we extend endless power and resources with no requirement that they answer to our elected officials or the taxpayers who fund their corruption? What else could we expect from an administration that spent eight years dancing to the globalists' drum?

A recent article that appeared in *The New American* published the following bold statement:

> "In the past, the CIA has been implicated in numerous scandals involving drug and weapons trafficking. From Vietnam and Iran to Latin America, the agency has repeatedly been caught importing narcotics and exporting arms for shadowy and subversive purposes."[121]

If you find it difficult to believe that American intelligence forces were not only involved in but acted as key players in drug trafficking operations, research every CIA director who has served (e.g. Henry Kissinger, Allen Dulles, George H. W. Bush, et. al.) since the CIA was created by the Council on Foreign Relations. You'll find evidence that all are entangled in similar activities. Here's the bottom line—the CFR and the CIA are organizations formed by the elites, of the elites, and exist for the purpose of serving the interests of the elites. Do they provide important sources of intel that are vital to national security and national defense? Yes. Would we be in grave danger without the information they provide to our leaders and military personnel? Absolutely! Does any of this mean that they're incapable of engaging in activities that are detrimental to American interests or those of the American people. No, it does not. Perhaps the old saying, "Can't live with 'em, can't live without 'em" is most applicable. Although some of the services they provide are indispensable, their corruption is something we can do without entirely, and it's time we stopped allowing it.

Considering the endless connections between Wall Street, multi-billion dollar international corporations, the elites, ruthless international cartels and our own intelligence forces, all of whom are shielded from exposure by corporate controlled media outlets leads to the conclusion that those we've entrusted have failed us. Accepting this does not require us to believe in a vast global conspiracy, nor does it become necessary for us to accuse all involved of evil intentions. We do, however, need to recognize the enemies that occupy the top tiers of the world's power structure, unite against them, and commit to a plan that prioritizes our interests going forward.

The cartels must be disbanded and those guilty of crimes must be punished. The global elites who profit from illegal activities that harm innocent people must be investigated and brought down. The traitors, sociopaths, and self-serving criminals that exist at every level of our government must be weeded out, punished, and replaced by honest, transparent people of good will who are subject to oversight and prosecution should personal greed ever lead them to betray their oaths or the public's trust. Finally, we must overhaul the news media, taking it out of the hands of corporations that are more committed to spreading globalist propaganda than they are reporting the truth. When media sources intentionally mislead us, they too must be held accountable. It's imperative that we act swiftly and decisively on all of these issues. The fate of the future of humanity rests in *our* hands!

CHAPTER 6

Up Close and Personal: Real Stories of Addiction

Statistics can't convey the human costs incurred or the very personal ways this epidemic has impacted countless victims and their families.   At this point, we shift our attention away from the numbers and the finger-pointing and zoom in on the experiences of a few everyday Americans whose lives have been torn apart by addiction. Their names have been changed to protect their identities. These are their true stories.

**A Story of Love and Loss: Jeremy & Aubrey
(California)**

I didn't recognize the number or the tearful voice on the other end of the phone who asked for me by name.

"Who is this?" I asked.

"My name is Ashley. I'm Aubrey's sister…Look, I know you'll probably hang up on me like the rest of her friends have, but I just had to try one more person."

"What can I do for you?" I asked reluctantly, knowing that the request could be literally anything under the sun given the out of control collision course with death Aubrey and her boyfriend, Jeremy, both good friends of mine, had been on as of late.

"My parents got a bill from the ambulance company. Aubrey and Jeremy were picked up by paramedics in Balboa Park. Both of them had overdosed and were unresponsive—flatlined. Somebody called and reported them—"

"My God, are they okay??" I interrupted.

"They're alive, they're certainly not okay. Look, my folks and I are really worried that the next call we get is going to be from the medical examiner to tell us my sister's dead. She's been avoiding us for weeks and we're worried sick. I was wondering if you knew where we might find her or if you could help us find her so we can try to help," the last few words of which were whispered as emotion had taken over her voice.

I didn't notice that the phone had fallen from my ear and was resting on my arm that was folded in front of me as thoughts raced through my head… "If I do this and Aubrey finds out, she'll never forgive me. But if I don't do it and something happens to that sweet, beautiful girl, I'll never forgive myself."

"Are you there?" I heard a muffled voice ask from the vicinity of my chest, so lost in the decision that for a split second I had forgotten that I was even on the phone.

"Yes, sorry. I'm here...I--I dropped the phone."

"Can you help us, please."

"Yes, I'll find her and bring her to my house, then I'll slip away from her and call you."

"Really?" she sounded a bit stunned that my agreement to cooperate had taken so little convincing, and a bit doubtful about my sincerity. Maybe she thought she had just been "okey-dokeyed" and would never actually hear from me.

"Yes, really. I want to help. It might take me a day or two to track her down, but as soon as I do, I'll call you, I promise."

"Thank you." She said in a voice that sounded like someone relieved, or pleading, or both.

It was already getting late, and I made a few calls and drove up University Avenue and back down El Cajon Blvd. a few times, hoping to just run across the two of them, but nothing. I went to bed feeling a bit relieved that I didn't find her. I was in no hurry to have my dear friend hate me, and that was sure to happen as soon as she became aware that I had tricked her into facing confrontation from her family.

Aubrey and Jeremy were both in their early 20s. From Jeremy's rugged but boyish good looks, ripped muscles, and deep southern accent, and Aubrey's loving, playful, childlike innocence, you'd never figure them to be living on the streets, becoming more dedicated to each other and their destructive addictions with each day that went by.

There was another big problem. You never saw either of them without the other one. They were inseparable. How would I do this for Aubrey's sister with Jeremy around? He'd be as furious as she was, maybe more. When I woke up the next morning, my friend and roommate Allen was coming in the back door.

The first thing he said to me was, "Did you hear Jeremy's dumb ass got arrested last night?"

"No, what happened?" I asked.

"Cops rolled up on 'em after Jeremy had loaded up a basket with food at Albertson's and charged the door. I guess they got a description and cops found him and Aubrey a couple blocks away making sandwiches out of the loot. They took him in for commercial burglary and he had some black and a couple points on him, so three new charges."

"Wow! Um…what about Aubrey? Did they take her too?' I asked.

"No, just him. They talked to her and told her she needed help and she needed to be away from him, but they let her go. She walked to Julie's house and stayed there for the rest of the night. I just came from over there. She's asleep on the floor."

"Oh, that's good," I said, not wanting to sound too excited and give my plan away, but knowing I needed to get over there in a hurry. It wouldn't be long until she would wake up and need a fix, and she'd be out making the rounds trying to get it.

Sure enough, she was already gone by the time I got there.

"Did she say where she was going?" I asked the guy on the couch who looked like he was in another world entirely. I had never seen him before.

"Not really," he said, never even looking up to make eye contact.

I spent the rest of the day looking for her. It was January, and even though San Diego has the best weather in the entire world, tonight it seemed unusually cold. I decided to swing by my house. The plan was to grab some coffee and a warm jacket and go right back out to continue looking for her. That wouldn't be necessary. As I pulled into my driveway, my headlights struck an image on the side of my house. Someone was looking in one of my windows. I'd know that gorgeous long, blonde hair anywhere.

We had only known each other as part of a larger group of friends for about a year, but the bond between us had formed quickly and effortlessly. She had an unbelievable calming effect on the people around her and an adorable sense of rebellion, both of which were oddly familiar and comforting to me. Our friendship had just clicked like a pair of old souls rediscovering each other for the fourth or fifth time.

As I walked toward her, I could see she was, or at least had been crying.

"What's up?" I asked, concerned.

"Jeremy got arrested and I'm out here on my own. Who knows how long he'll be locked up this time?"

"Come on in, let's figure it all out," I said reassuringly.

Could I really do this to her right now? She was already feeling defeated. Calling her sister and having this go down tonight might just send her over the edge. Oh well, I thought, I promised, and this is a window of opportunity to get it done while Jeremy was gone for a couple days.

The hell I had been though with these two was extensive. If you're my friend, I'm there for you no matter what. They would happen by once in a while and ask if they could take a shower. After they'd been in the bathroom for over an hour, I'd start to panic, thinking there might be more going on in there than just some private affection, so I stood outside the door and listened. Hearing nothing but water hitting water, I'd start banging on the door. Jeremy would fling the door open and then look at her. She was unresponsive. Her skin was turning blue. He started screaming her name and hitting her in the face with an open first. Finally, she would gasp for air and look up at him, still immobilized, but with just enough wherewithal to utter the word, "Stop!" in reference to the repeated blows he was delivering to try to bring her back.

"What the *hell*, man?! I said I didn't want you guys doing that stuff here, and I'm *serious*!" I took it personally. I felt like I had been disrespected, and I had been, but this was before I realized that it wasn't about me at all. My feelings had no place in the minds of two devout heroin addicts. Don't get me wrong, they meant me no harm, but as I would later come to understand, it was all about avoiding the debilitating sickness of "kickin,'" (a.k.a. withdrawals).

There was also the night they had been arguing and Jeremy came over by himself. I was leaving about the time he showed up. He looked super depressed.

"I'll be right back. Just walking down to the corner store. Do you want me to get you anything?" I asked.

"Nah, I'm good, but can I get a spoon before you go?"

"Of course," I answered, actually thinking he was going to eat some ice cream or frozen yogurt or something. To me, that was what people needed spoons for, right? This time I couldn't have been more wrong.

When I got back from the store which couldn't have been more than 10 minutes later, I could hear the voice of Rosemary, one of the ladies that lived next door coming from my garage.

"NO, JEREMY! You're NOT gonna do this to me you MOTHER FU—ER!!" The sound of skin slapping skin told me that whatever was going on had quickly escalated from a verbal altercation to a more physical one. I pulled the door open wondering what on earth could be going on. There was his lifeless body lying on the floor of my garage. Rosemary was trying like hell to wake him up.

Together we dragged him out to the sidewalk. I immediately checked for a pulse. Feeling none, I started rescue breathing and chest compressions. Allen suggested calling 911, an idea I was not in favor of since we had just moved into that house a few days earlier, and I couldn't see how having a fleet of emergency response vehicles show up at my address would be an ideal way to introduce myself to my new neighbors.

I continued CPR. After about a minute of getting no response, I asked someone from the growing crowd of bystanders who were beginning to congregate to summon paramedics. I worked with him until I saw the crash truck come around the corner, then left it to the pros who were able to stabilize him quickly. Of course, the next day he was apologetic and embarrassed, which was little consolation to me after a night of what I considered to be pure lunacy.

At that point I realized that the overdose victims are the ones who have the least insight. After all, they are usually unconscious, more than likely floating on a cloud while everyone else is in total meltdown mode trying to figure out what to do. They get to miss all of that. To add insult to injury, they usually wake up angry with rescuers for "ruining their high." They're also cranky because they're "dope sick." No matter what I said or how frustrated I was, this wouldn't be the last time I would be expected to rise to such an occasion for these two.

It was hard to stay angry with them. Not only had they both been my friends prior to becoming addicts, they were just two of the most charming people I had ever known. Jeremy, who was raised in Tennessee and Alabama, had such a magnetic personality. His perpetual smile and laidback, accepting, southern style made people gravitate toward him and trust him. To me, it was shameful that heroin was changing all of that.

Aubrey was an absolute ray of light. Her smile could melt the glaciers. Her loyalty was unyielding. Born and raised in San Diego County, she was a California girl through and through. She had many talents, was naturally radiant and had an unassuming naivete about her that made her all the more stunning. Was there any way to help these two who loved life, loved their friends, loved each other, but were destroying all that was good in their lives for their love of heroin?

It was time to get it over with. After she and I talked for a few minutes, I told her it had been a long day and I wanted to relax in a hot shower. I slipped into the bathroom and called Ashley. She answered right away.

"She's here, at my house right now," I said. "The address is 3912 Polk in City Heights if you want to come and talk with her right now."

"It's not actually me who's going to be coming. I'm sending my husband, Jerry. He has a really good rapport with Aubrey, and I think he has the best chance of getting through to her."

"That's fine." I whispered.

"Thank you so much! You have no idea how much we appreciate it." she said and hung up the phone.

When I heard the doorbell ring about 20 minutes later, I went and let him in.

"Aubrey," I said, bringing Jerry into the room where she had been sitting since we got there, "there's somebody here to see you."

"Oh my God, Jerry? Wait…Nooooo! How did you find me here?" Big tears were beginning to well up in her eyes.

"Yeah, you can blame me for that," I said. "I'm sorry, but your family is worried about you, and to me this seemed like the right thing to do, so if you're going to be mad at anyone, be mad at me. I'm gonna go in my room and let you guys talk…just talk. It's okay."

A minute later, she was hugging Jerry, crying, but holding on to him tightly, still saying, "Nooo, what are you doing here? I can't. I just can't."

He stayed for a couple hours, until well after midnight. Although I was doing my best not to eavesdrop, it was clear that he was cajoling her to leave with him and go check into a treatment facility. She was as determined to stay as he was to take her. I was relieved that they had a nice visit and that she wasn't mad at me, but I had hoped she would go with him and get help. I was truly worried about both of them, and while I didn't have to worry about Jeremy on that particular night, I knew that the extremely liberal local laws and the overworked criminal court system in San Diego County were two factors that would come together causing him to be released within a day or two.

Jerry came back the next day. Jeremy got out of jail the next day. It was their first meeting and there was obviously tension. Jeremy had no interest in going to treatment. He had just been locked up and had one thing on his mind. Jerry would extend the offer to get both of them help, seeing as how Aubrey's loyalty to Jeremy seemed to be her biggest excuse for not wanting to go. Jerry left disappointed, but he would come back many times over the next several months. He turned out to be an incredibly decent man who would give me money and gift cards to feed them, not wanting to give them cash that might be used for drugs that would kill them. Neither of us could have that on our consciences, so we had an unspoken deal that went on for quite some time. I have to say I was very impressed with Jerry's patience and persistence. He never gave up.

One of the ladies next door was taking an advanced film course at a local college. She had an assignment to produce a short, silent film. She and her partner Rosemary had taken quite an interest in Jeremy and Aubrey, and it was decided that her film would be called, "The Turning Point." It would feature Jeremy and Aubrey and their addiction. She asked if they could film part of it in my garage. I agreed, not really thinking anything would come out of it, but something did.

Aubrey was contacted by a lady who said she was making a documentary about heroin addiction. She offered to pay her and Jeremy for participating in two filmed interviews and a photoshoot. They were excited about the opportunity to earn some legitimate cash in a way that wouldn't require doing any shoplifting or anything "shady."

A few nights later, Aubrey showed up at my house in tears. She was starting to have withdrawals and Jeremy was nowhere in sight. She told me he had just been arrested for trying to steal a bike from someone on the trolley. Apparently, the guy had put up a fight and Jeremy assaulted him. The bad news for him was that the entire incident had been caught on camera.

In San Diego, if you commit a minor crime, you go home. If the crime causes harm to someone, you go to jail. With Jeremy's other minor crimes, he was starting to become known to local cops and the City Attorney's office. It looked like he might actually serve a few months in jail this time. Aubrey was truly devastated. I did something that was compassionate but very much out of character for me. I drove her to her dealer's house and bought her enough heroin to stave off the sickness that was coming over her. We went back to my house and after she did her small dose, she became very relaxed and comfortable. We sat up all night laughing and having one of our best talks ever. When the sun came up, she thanked me and apologized that she had to go. She had the photoshoot appointment at a hotel downtown. Even though she wasn't sure if they wanted her to come alone, and although it wouldn't be the same without Jeremy, she went, thinking they might want to proceed with just her. I hugged her tightly, not knowing I wouldn't see her again for more than a year.

Later that day, my next door neighbor came to share some exciting news. It turned out that the photoshoot Aubrey had gone to that morning wasn't a photoshoot at all. She entered the room and saw the lights and camera crew she was expecting to see, but there were other people there she definitely hadn't counted on. Her mother, father, both of her sisters and Jerry were seated and there was one empty chair for her. There was a camera crew from the A&E network along with a family counselor they had provided. Aubrey had been tricked. She and her family were to be among the first to participate in the network's new series, *Intervention*.

The somber faces of her family members told her that this was no joke. She was confronted by each one individually, and asked, "Will you go get help today?" At first, she became very defensive, lashed out at all of them, and vehemently rejected the idea. Her sister was overcome with emotion and had to excuse herself from the room. Everyone else stood strong and gave her a series of ultimatums. The network had agreed to pay the tab for her to go to Miami to one of the nation's best treatment centers. All of the arrangements had been made, including a private jet that was waiting at Lindbergh Field to whisk her off to Florida. All she had to do was agree to go. It took almost two hours, countless tears, and overcoming a myriad of excuses, but she ultimately agreed to go.

I felt elated that this had happened. I felt proud of the split second decision I had made when Aubrey's sister had called me. It might have been the first step of a process that saved her life. A letter came from Miami about two weeks later. The tone expressed wasn't at all what I expected. Aubrey was furious that she had been tricked. She was miserable about the decision she had made. She was livid with her parents. She demanded a ticket back to California, vowing to hitchhike if no one would provide it. I sat down and wrote a 30-page letter back to her. It broke the entire situation down, from my point-of-view and from her family's perspective. I begged her to give the program a full month before deciding if she really wanted to leave.

It was a long time before I heard anything else from her, but I had spoken with Jerry who told me that she was settling into the program and doing extremely well. Jeremy was released from jail to a twelve-step program in Riverside County. Rumor had it that he was also on the straight and narrow. After everything I endured with these two, it did my heart good to see that both had found their way into recovery, even if that meant they couldn't be together for a period of time. How much time was anybody's guess. Would they both stay clean? Would sobriety change the dynamics of their relationship if they were to eventually end up back in the same city?

Jeremy excelled in his program. There was nothing he couldn't do when he was sober. People adored him, and the doors of opportunity were wide open. Once he finished the program, the facility hired him on as a staff member who mentored new admits and helped them through their orientation phase—undoubtedly their toughest time, but he was good at it. He was good at anything and everything he put his mind to. He made a mistake by getting involved with a female client—a big no-no in recovery settings. When confronted about the relationship, he relapsed. The program administrators liked him so much that they offered to hold his job for him if he would go through the program again as a patient.

He started back at square one, but quickly became discouraged. How does one go from being everybody's favorite staff member, trusted with freedom and authority, back to having endless restrictions and no privileges? Memories of the brief taste of freedom he had during his relapse started to seem sweeter. The first time he got a pass to go off grounds for a probation appointment, he ditched the staff member he was with and fled back to San Diego. He immediately resumed his addict lifestyle, but he was on his own now, as Aubrey was still in Miami.

She got in touch with me when she came back after more than a year. There was no doubt in anyone's mind that she was transformed. Not only had she gone through the best treatment money could buy, she had really applied herself, worked the steps, and was ready to come home. When

Jeremy heard that she was back, he wanted to see her immediately. She was disappointed to learn that he had fallen back into his old ways, which was a deal-breaker for her. She refused to see him, citing her own sobriety as just too important to risk. He was devastated and sank deeper into his habit.

A near fatal overdose landed him in the hospital for almost a week. His mother, Elise, flew out from South Carolina to be with him as he recovered. Because he had violated probation and continued to engage in crimes to support his habit, the judge sentenced him to time in the state prison. Elise flew out from the east coast again, begging the court to let her take him home with her, but the judge refused to grant him permission to leave the state of California.

As Aubrey got settled back into a normal life, surrounded by family and friends who loved and supported her, she started thinking about Jeremy. She knew she had always loved him, and decided she wanted to see him whenever he got released from prison. The only condition was that he would have to be sober. She got his number from a mutual friend, but not until he had already been out for a few days. She tried calling him many times over several days, but he never answered or returned her calls. This made no sense to her as he had wanted so much to see her before he went to prison. She called me to ask me if I had heard from him. I had not, and to be honest, I didn't encourage her to keep reaching out. Everyone was so proud of her success and no one wanted to see her get dragged back down.

About three weeks passed. Two of my good friends, Candace and Selena came by to visit. I hadn't seen them in a while, and we were in the process of catching up on lost time. Jeremy's name came up. I think I was the one who brought it up in the context of whatever memory or old story we were talking about. A grave look suddenly came over Selena's face. "I heard he died," she said. "I'm not sure if it's true, but I heard something happened to him about a month ago."

"What?!" I yelled, shocked and horrified. "God, no! You can't be serious!"

She repeated that she wasn't sure, but I was already on the computer typing his name into Google search. A link came up to a funeral home in South Carolina. I figured he had a pretty common first, middle, and last name, so maybe the exact match I had found was a coincidence. It just had to be a coincidence. I held my breath as I clicked on the link. Seconds later, I was looking at a page that had his picture prominently displayed next to an image of a burning candle and the words, "Forever rest in peace."

My heart sank lower than I knew it could. My first thought was, "This just can't be. He just turned 30 years old." This was immediately replaced by my second thought, "Somebody has got to reach out to his mother!" I had never met Elise but had heard so much about her and knew that she and her son had a very special relationship and that she must be devastated beyond words.

It was 2:30 in the morning, but I went out and bought her a sympathy card and some stationary. I didn't know her address, but felt I absolutely had to reach out to her. I decided to send the card to the funeral home with a request asking them to please forward it to the family. The letter I wrote was four or five pages long. I expressed my heartfelt sympathy, told her how much she had meant to her son, and offered to make a memorial video to celebrate his life. What mattered most to me in communicating with her was to help her feel better about her son's life, understanding that nothing I could say would make her feel any better about his death. I wanted her to know that his life wasn't all about drugs and partying, that he actually had some decent people in California who truly cared about him, and that he lived well among friends who never turned him away. I had no idea what her reaction would be. My hands were shaking as I sealed the envelope and dropped it in the mailbox. It wouldn't have been the first time someone had been offended by my truest of intentions, but I felt compelled to make contact even if the response was not positive, even if there was no response at all.

As I waited for a reply, I spent a lot of time talking with Aubrey. She was beyond crushed. We learned during the days that followed that Jeremy had been released from prison and had gone to a resort hotel in Mission Valley with a group of friends. According to the police, everyone at the party was loaded, especially Jeremy. He was allegedly being loud and disruptive around the pool area, attracting what his friends thought was the wrong kind of attention to the group. Later we would find out that this was simply their excuse for cleaning up the room and leaving once they realized he had overdosed. They panicked thinking there was nothing else they could do. Jeremy was found the following morning.

He had been dead for several hours. The air conditioning unit in the room had been turned up.

The night this happened was the same night Aubrey had started calling his number, leaving messages. She continued to call for several days, but Jeremy's phone was in an evidence locker at the police department as the investigation into his death was conducted. She cried uncontrollably about the tragic timing of events. She blamed herself for not calling him sooner, thinking she could have saved him. I can't express how hard it was to see my beautiful friend of whom I was so proud shaming and punishing herself for something that wasn't even remotely her fault.

I made a point of making myself available to her anytime she needed to talk. I prayed that this wouldn't trigger her to fall off the wagon. I wished I had been at that party too. I certainly wouldn't have left him there to die. I didn't understand how his "friends" could abandon him as they did. I had brought him back several times in the past and would always value a friend's life above any possibility of getting myself in trouble. That kind of selfishness was just foreign to me. As I listened to Aubrey cry and torment herself, all I could think was, "If only I had been there!"

About a week had passed since I had mailed the letter and card to Elise. I woke up on Thanksgiving Day and found the following e-mail in my inbox:

A Mother's Love: A Letter from Elise, Jeremy's mom (South Carolina)

"I cannot express to you enough the gratitude for your letter......I came home yesterday from a trip from Birmingham and Nashville and there it was.

I read it three times yesterday and twice (so far) today......it does make me cry; however, I am sooooooo thankful for your kind and heartfelt words. I would very much like to talk to you......bad day today, will have to wait on that, OK?

I know that my precious son is FINALLY at peace....no more struggles....no more pain. There is no one in this world that deserves that more than Jeremy. One phrase that I have loved to keep in my heart: no more sleeping on the cold hard ground, now on puffy white clouds!

I am not so sure this email is easy for you to read....
it's being typed through hard tears. I know that he
did not like tears.... he will just have to put up with a
few for a while!

Thank you for all that you have done in the past to
help Jeremy and all that you are doing now. All of
"his girls" are planning a trip to Cali sometime after
the holidays......I can hardly wait to meet you!!

I would very much like to stay in touch with you!!! I
understand that you are helping Aubrey....thank you
for that.... never met her but know she loved
Jeremy....talked with her a few times.

Until we "talk" again, Elise."

About 2 months later, Elise made that difficult trip to
California where a small gathering of close friends was held
in the meeting room of a local hotel. Her daughter, Jeremy's
sister, accompanied her. Together, we would all spend an
afternoon sharing memories, consoling one another, and
celebrating his 30 years of life on earth.

Aubrey gave a tearful speech in which she listed some of his missed possibilities: "Jeremy could have been an athlete, a rock star, a businessman, a model…" I desperately wanted Elise to know that Jeremy's life in California had meaning. It wasn't filled with shallow, superficial people. He never spent a single night hungry and on the streets. I took her to the hotel where he spent his last night. I wanted her to see that it wasn't the dark, dirty, drug-infested hell hole that she might have envisioned, but a bright, clean, resort-style establishment in San Diego's premiere hotel district. She was very brave, facing this and every aspect of her loss head-on. I looked on thinking that if there was any comfort I could bring to this grief-stricken mother whose heart I knew was broken forever, I wanted to provide it.

Ten years have now passed. Elise and her husband Ben remain close friends of mine to this day. I have visited them several times in South Carolina. They welcome me into their home where I sleep in Jeremy's room with everything still arranged exactly as he left it the last time he was home. She tells me, "you keep my precious son's memory alive, and I simply love you!" She will never be the same as she was before. None of us will. In many ways, she has moved on, healed by the years that have passed, and fortified by the fact that she is a woman of unbreakable strength who has lived each day determined to overcome the most heart wrenching ordeal a mother could ever know.

Aubrey, too, has moved on. She now lives in Indiana and has two beautiful children. The years, however, have been hard for her. She's had trouble with intimacy after losing the love of her life, and the timing of events as they occurred have haunted her for more than a decade now. She is also saved by the fact that she's very strong—much stronger than even she knows. I thank God that she has never gone back to heroin. In fact, she calls me every year on her "clean date" to tell me she loves me and to thank me for making that call that began her road to recovery. Getting that call is always a proud moment, as is every time I hear from Elise and notice the gradual progress she has made in the wake of a tragedy that turned her life upside-down. They're both amazing women, and we all share a bond that will last forever.

I have only one regret—that we weren't able to save Jeremy. The years of life that he lost weigh heavy on all of our hearts. "Why did this have to happen to him?" is a question now echoed by thousands of American families who have been ravaged by this epidemic. This is the story of how one precious, young life was lost, and others were profoundly affected by the chaos that ensues when drugs take over. Please pray for our nation, for the sons and daughters, mothers and fathers, sisters and brothers, and the dear friends who are left behind by those who had to say goodbye long before it should have been their time.

Shattered Dreams: Rachel's Story
(Virginia)

The story of Rachel's upbringing is about as normal as can be. She was the youngest of three girls, born to a father who was retired from the U.S. Army and had served in the Korean War, and a stay at home mom who took care of all things domestic. The family lived a happy, middle class life near an army base in North Carolina. The desire to be closer to her maternal grandmother whose health was starting to decline prompted the family to move to Northern Virginia. Rachel, a freshman in high school, started thinking about a career path. Upon graduating from high school, she continued living at home, worked as a telemarketer, and volunteered for the local rescue squad. She declared nursing as her major when she entered community college.

She had a small circle of close friends who loved to drink on the weekends, often to excess, but drugs were not, nor did she ever imagine they would be a part of her life. She was always very close to her parents even when she moved out and shared a townhouse with her two closest girlfriends. She had a bit of a wild streak, a trait she shared with some of her closest friends. At times they got rowdy and brought out the worst in each other, but never anything serious. Again, her future was without any foreseeable constraints, and her everyday life was as normal as any God-fearing American girl's could be.

Eventually she met the man she would marry, a local guy who sold used cars and held various other jobs in addition to volunteering on the local rescue squad. Rachel got a decent full-time job offer working for an ambulance company and decided to put college on hold for the time being. For the first couple years of her marriage, she was living the dream—the life she had always imagined. Although the couple was saddened to learn that they weren't able to have children together, they moved past that and focused on each other and their careers. Her relationship with her parents had never been stronger. They'd take short trips on the weekends and she loved sharing recipes and decorating and craft ideas with her mom. No matter how old she got, she was always daddy's little girl. He was her hero and never stopped being fiercely protective of her.

Suddenly, things started to get challenging. She was diagnosed with lupus and degenerative disc disease—herniated disks. Doctors treated the pain with opiates that kept her able to function and work. There was much to be excited about as her husband had entered a new business venture that was really taking off. Before long, the two of them were running the most successful crime-scene clean up business in the mid-Atlantic region. Soon they were clearing six figures and living the good life. Then she got some news that would change her life forever.

Her beloved mother was diagnosed with advanced pancreatic cancer—the deadliest form of cancer that exists, with a five year survival prognosis of less that 1 percent. In fact, the vast majority of patients are not alive one year after diagnosis. Based on the position and progression of her cancer, her mom was only given a few months. Rachel rose to the task of being her mom's primary caregiver, seeing to it that her needs were met and that she could stay home and pass into the afterlife in comfortable, familiar surroundings. Hospice came to provide in-home services, but it was Rachel who was there the biggest part of the time. As heartbreaking as it was, she felt honored to do it. Somehow, her mother held on for almost nine months, declining a little more each day. Rachel put her own needs behind her mother's and never realized that the pain medications she was taking were providing just a little bit of a crutch through the tough weeks at the end.

Around the time she buried her mom, there were more health problems brewing. A rare disease was causing the flow of blood to erode the bone tissue in both of her feet. Reconstructive surgery would hopefully repair the damage and get her back on her feet again. Of course, this meant more pain, stronger pain medication, and more of it. Three months had not passed since her mother had died when more terrible news came. This time it was her father--stage 4 lung cancer that had spread to his bones. He, too, would require total care for the little time he had left. Again, Rachel stepped up to the plate and faithfully served her other parent right up until his last breath. It doesn't matter how strong someone is. Losing both parents within a year of each other is just plain hard. Thank God she still had her marriage and the business was doing well.

Rachel and her husband decided to buy a new home. With the money they were making and the lump sum her parents had left her, they were able to close on a beautiful new four-bedroom place in a newly developed suburban community. They had spent much of the money that was coming in from the business buying cars and covering Rachel's mounting medical bills, so she agreed to sink all of her inheritance into the down payment on their home, which left enough to furnish it in style, including a fully stocked paper craft room where she could enjoy working on one of her favorite hobbies.

Her health continued to decline. On top of her physical ailments, Rachel found herself in a period of deep depression, most likely brought on by the grief of losing both parents. She missed them terribly. The new house in all of its splendor ended up being a source of more depression from the beginning. What was the point of having a beautiful place to live if her folks weren't there to see it and share in the pride? There were more surgeries on her foot, then secondary infections. She was in and out of the emergency room, had numerous hospital admissions. Dilaudid, Morphine, and Oxycontin were routinely included in the treatment plans.

For the first time her husband who had been so supportive through it all seemed distant. He spent many hours away from home, presumably working. Money from the business was disappearing almost as fast as it came in. Her heart sank when she discovered that he had developed a compulsive gambling problem, but the disappointment that brought didn't hold a candle to the despair she felt when she finally confirmed her worst fear. He was having an affair and had the audacity to feel justified in his actions, blaming his wandering eye on her depression and insisting that she wasn't "fun to be around" anymore. Apparently, he didn't take the sacred vows "for better or for worse, in sickness and in health" very seriously.

To say Rachel was devastated is a tremendous understatement. Her marriage was essentially over, the finances were in disarray, and more foot reconstruction would be needed, but two toes would have to be amputated. The pain in her foot was unbearable at times and despite the doctors increasing her pain prescriptions to what were reaching dangerous levels, they were barely taking the edge off of the agony she felt with every step. One thing did not occur to her at the time, however—the fact that opiates were essentially the only thing bringing her any comfort or relief, not just in terms of her physical suffering, but they were masking a great deal of the emotional pain too. This is exactly how addiction establishes itself in the life of an innocent and unsuspecting person. It approaches gradually. Its mere presence is deceiving. It soothes as it quietly demands more. It makes the unbearable bearable, as long as the flow remains steady.

Months went by. Bills went unpaid, but prescriptions continued to be filled. Rachel worked full-time in the business office of a successful auto repair shop, but her salary wasn't even a fraction of what was needed to keep up with the expenses. Her husband broke every promise to her, including the one to keep the house payments current. She filed for divorce around the time the bank served notice that their home was in foreclosure. She would have to find the money for the mortgage or get out.

Taking the pills orally no longer seemed to be killing the pain in her foot, which had been reconstructed twice, and the bones were set with a giant metal contraption she called a "tomato cage" that kept everything in place. She found that she got a little more relief by crushing the pills and snorting them. Anything that controlled the excruciating pain in her foot was worth trying. She was on her way home one night when the police stopped her because a taillight on her car had burned out. The officer shined his flashlight into her car and saw a short straw she had cut to inhale her medications. He searched the car and conducted a field sobriety test. She was taken to jail and charged with DUI for driving under the influence of her pain meds. She knew you could get arrested and charged for drinking and driving or driving under while impaired by recreational drugs, but for prescription medicine? It didn't seem fair, nor did the license suspension or thousands of dollars in fines she faced for the violation.

There were months when it was hard to afford her medication and have money left for food. She had a friend who also suffered from chronic pain who solicited her to trade some of her pills for the cash she needed to make ends meet. She did this a few times and it seemed like no big deal. After delivering the pills one day, she was stopped at gunpoint by the state police. The officer's demeanor and stern command for her to get out of the car told her immediately that this was no routine traffic stop. She had been targeted in a statewide narcotics sting operation and had unwittingly sold Schedule 1 narcotics to an undercover police officer several times. She was taken to county jail and charged with four felony counts of narcotics sales, each carrying up to nine years in the state prison. Her car was confiscated immediately. The only attorney she could afford to represent her assured her that there was no way out of a lengthy prison sentence. This was all complicated by the fact that the charges were also a violation of the probation she was still under for the DUI. She was told that she wouldn't be eligible for any form of house arrest because state minimum sentence laws required mandatory custody for "drug dealers."

The entire nightmare was so surreal. How could they label her a drug dealer? She had innocently traded some pills with a friend, but in the eyes of the law she was no different from a thug pushing heroin in an elementary schoolyard. How did this happen? How did she go from being daddy's girl who worked accidents and crime scenes with police as a first responder to an addict charged with multiple drug-related felonies for which she faced unimaginable years in prison? The drugs she got were from her doctor. She had legitimate pain issues. She never thought of herself as a criminal. How had everything gotten so crazy in such a short period of time?

All the while her foot continued to throb. She missed her parents more than ever. As she was herded through the criminal justice process, she knew they would not provide her pain medications in prison. The pain and the withdrawals would be more severe than she could imagine and there would be absolutely no mercy from the prison staff. Suicide seemed to be the only way out of her impossible situation. She hated the idea of ending her life but hated the prospect of the enormous suffering that was inevitably ahead of her even more. Things had never seemed so hopeless. She found a sliver of relief in melting her prescriptions down and injecting them. She never thought of herself as a junkie, but it didn't matter anyway. This was the way she planned to go out of this world peacefully the night before she would have to report for her sentence.

Despite the gravity of her situation, her close friends begged her not to give up, insisting that judges, too, are human, that justice is compassionate, and that the courts would surely take her life circumstances into account when handing down her sentence. Honestly, they had no idea if this would turn out to be true but said whatever they could to convince her to hold on. A lifelong friend who lived on the other side of the country wrote a thoughtful letter to the judge on her behalf. It detailed the horrors of her story, begged for mercy, and voiced concerns that she might take her own life. There was no reason to have any hope whatsoever based on everything she had been told by the courts and her attorney as each appearance brought her closer to her dreaded sentencing dates. Her friends prayed harder than they had ever prayed for anything before.

The sentence imposed would not be easy, but the prayers, letters, and months of encouragement paid off. She was ordered to pay thousands of dollars in fines, and her sentence would be followed by many years of probation, but by the sheer grace of God, the judge took compassion on her soul and allowed her to serve her three year sentence at home! Halleluiah! There would be mandatory check-ins with the probation department. She would have to answer daily phone calls which required her to blow into an alcohol-detection device. She would also need to schedule advanced permission to attend doctor appointments and shop for groceries. With those exceptions, she would be a prisoner in her own home for the next three years. It didn't seem like much of a reason to celebrate, but considering what could have happened, she was overjoyed.

She knew she was addicted to opiates, but that knowledge had become a normal part of life. Because she had chronic pain from a host of incurable conditions, her doctors had told her she could expect to be on these medications for the rest of her life. She struggled through the house arrest period. The state had suspended her driver license and never returned the vehicle they seized when she was first arrested. Support from a man she was establishing a new relationship with, in addition to her disability benefits made it possible to squeak by each month, still facing huge fines that she would be required to pay when allowed to start working again, but at least she was not in prison. Thank God! At least she was not in constant pain and could keep getting the medicines she totally depended upon to get through every hour.

Eventually, the three year sentence was over. She could come and go as she pleased, but seven years of probation and money she owed loomed over her head and absorbed every penny she had coming in. The drugs, which she was allowed to use because they were duly prescribed, continued to provide her only source of comfort and relief. Dictated by the tolerance built up over many years, the amount of opiate medication she consumes today is unbelievable. Sometimes, when her prescriptions run out before she can refill them at the end of the month, she has to find other sources of opiates to prevent going through unmanageable withdrawals. Her last option is street heroin, a scary prospect, but not as daunting as the thought of having to live without anything.

Rachel's story is not unique. She is one of millions of Americans who function marginally despite their daily use of and dependence on opiate drugs. She has made recent attempts to reduce her intake, understanding the risks of overdose. Still, her friends helplessly pace the floors, wringing their hands worrying that one day she'll cross that line, do a little too much, or get a bad batch. But as it stands now, there are no viable solutions to her problems. It's hard for most of us to imagine the choice between living every minute of every day with the worst pain we've ever known and having to take massive quantities of deadly drugs in order to get some control of it. As Americans, however, most of us now know the pain of mourning a family member or friend we've lost to this epidemic. Most of us also know someone who lives as a functioning addict, so we worry, we hope, and we live, in the greatest country in the world, and pray every day for miracles.

Trey
(Washington)

Nobody saw this coming…nobody!

Trey was a stunning young man. His high cheekbones and rows of bright white, perfectly formed teeth gave him that million-dollar smile that he always wore with pride. That along with his floppy, carefree skater boy hair that crashed down over his huge, bright green eyes made everyone give him a second look. But it wasn't all about looks with Trey. Don't get me wrong. It meant everything to him to be immaculate in appearance, but his natural good looks made that part of his life effortless. It was a given, and as anyone who broke through his exterior found out quickly, there was so much more to him.

Trey had depth. He grew up as a preacher's son in a small conservative town in central Washington. Being an outstanding student was also effortless as God had blessed him with unusually high intelligence. Although trouble erupted between his parents when he was a little boy, his mother, a nurse, U.S. Air Force veteran, and faithful follower of Jesus, was overflowing with love for Trey and his younger brother. The fact that he was gay changed none of that.

As a teenager, Trey was popular among his peers and got into the things adolescents in small towns got into in the first decade of the 2000s. Cigarettes, alcohol, pot here and there. From a wide-eyed, precocious child to a tenacious but well-mannered teen, he learned everything he was supposed to learn quickly, which left much time to wonder about everything else. Poised for one of the brightest futures a young man could have and driven more by the hormones and curiosity that rule every man when he comes of age than occasionally butting heads with his step-father, he set out for Seattle.

Of course, the big city opened its arms to Trey, as did the LGBT community in all of its splendor. His plans for college and dreams of success were never abandoned, just temporarily put on hold while he experienced the club scene, the night life, and an enormous community of confident gay men of every shape, size, color, and walk of life who were comfortable in their own skin and more than eager to accept him. Viewed against the small-town life he came from, he was mesmerized and thought he had found nirvana. He was in a hurry to experience it all—the relationships, the sex, the parties. It was his time to shine and live the life that just didn't seem to exist back home.

After a few months in Seattle, Trey settled into a group of friends close to his age, mostly other good-looking, innocent gay "boys" between seventeen and nineteen years old. They were always invited to parties and were no strangers to being preyed upon by older men. There was one man in his forties who especially liked guys around Trey's age. He had money, a lavish home, and lots of drugs to keep the younger men coming around. He never told any of them that he was HIV positive. They all got infected, Trey getting his diagnosis at the tender age of eighteen. He felt scared and betrayed by the tremendous injustice that had been done to him. He didn't realize it at the time, but a part of him was forgetting the dreams he had growing up. The AIDS virus made his future uncertain at best. It also ended his dream of having children and locked him into being gay forever. After all, he believed, any possibility of marrying a woman or settling into a "normal" life was now gone. The only escape from these realities seemed to be more drugs and allowing himself to sink deeper into the hedonistic lifestyle.

One thing led to another and Trey ended up in California with a man a couple decades his senior. He kept in close contact with his mom who worried about him constantly and prayed for him daily as it was his practice to share with her the intimate details of his life which, she admits, were more than she ever wanted to know. Days turned into weeks which rolled by and became years. There was something missing, something he was searching for. Love? Genuine fulfillment? Lasting satisfaction? These were elements of life that didn't seem to exist in the "party and play" lifestyle that he found himself submerged in.

In the superficial world where virtuous people are scarce and deep emotions are numbed with multiple sex partners, methamphetamines, ecstasy, and GHB, Trey was looking for whatever it was that was missing. He bounced around until he got involved with another older man who took him in. Their relationship was intense but turbulent, but he had found someone he loved who stimulated him intellectually, cooked his dinner every night, and kept him going with an endless supply of drugs.

He made a lot of fair-weather friends, mostly gay men who took one look at him and proceeded with an eye toward sexual conquest. He partied, day and night, always looking for something more, but never exactly sure what it was, or if he'd even know if he were to find it. In his vast circle of acquaintances, he managed to forge a couple of lasting friendships—decent people who saw his inner beauty and cared for his soul. He gravitated toward them and treated them with great respect.

Despite the chaos and scandal that dominated the lives of many he surrounded himself with, he was always a very decent person, even in the most difficult of times. He approached the people in his life with a gentle kindness. He loved animals, flowers, and babies. He hated violence, cruelty, and oppression. Some called him an "old soul." Others referred to him as "good people." Everyone agreed, however, that he was very special, and that to know him was to love him.

Although Trey prided himself at being "emotionally unavailable," anyone with a hint of basic people skills could see that he was not. His thoughts ran deep. His pain ran deep. He was tired. Life was passing him by without giving him something he longed for. But what was it? There was a passion that burned deep inside him, an incorrigible sense of right and wrong, and a ferocious obsession with social justice. He loved to debate, and despite the fact that his aspirations of higher education had been put on hold, he could argue with the best and spoke like a Harvard scholar. His knowledge of history, science, religion, and philosophy floored those with enough depth to engage in discussions with him. He was the entire package. Good looks, humility, global awareness, and a kind, loyal, and loving spirit. Even though he didn't have much, he was generous, always shared what he had, and never judged anyone.

If anything was ever certain, it was that Trey did not belong on the dead-end road that had become his life, and he knew it. After 4 years in California, he did the hardest thing someone in his position could do. He turned his back on all of it, boarded a plane, and went home. His parents and grandparents were thrilled. It seemed that their endless prayers to protect him and deliver him through the storm had finally paid off.

After a few days of hibernating through the detox phase, he started to rebuild his life. He quit smoking, stopped drinking, and swore off drugs. He developed a four year plan that included a part-time job and some college courses to get his feet wet. He ate three (sometimes four) meals a day, and put on fifty pounds, which made him look healthy by bringing out the glow that drugs had stolen from him. He spent a lot of time with his mom, going on frequent walks with her to Starbucks where they would sit and talk about everything and nothing at the same time—making memories that she will undoubtedly cherish until she takes her last breath.

He had been home, and sober, for about 6 months. To his family, it seemed things couldn't be going better. Trey was back, on the road to recovery, and visions of that bright future they had always known was in store for him seemed more realistic than ever. Trey had always struggled with issues of faith despite the strong influence instilled in him by his parents and the church as he was growing up. He unabashedly questioned, sometimes flat-out rejected, and occasionally scorned the customs and traditions of organized religion, despite being an obviously very spiritual person. Finally, it became clear that he was, in fact, a believer when news came that a friend had been diagnosed with advanced lung cancer. He asked his mom to pray with him for that friend, and so they did.

A couple months later, a package came in the mail addressed to Trey. His eyes lit up as he grabbed it and hurried into his room, closing the door behind him. The details of the 24 hours that followed are somewhat unclear and may never be known. His grandmother thought he was behaving strangely but didn't want to pry or invade the young man's privacy. After all, he had been doing so well. He didn't show up for work the following morning but made a rather bizarre phone call to his job telling his manager, "I didn't think you guys wanted me there." He was told to come in, and that they not only wanted but needed him there. He agreed to come in, but never arrived.

Later that day, in the early afternoon, paramedics responded to a call that there was a young man having a seizure on a nature trail that runs between the town and the river. They arrived to find Trey unresponsive and with a body temperature of 106F degrees. They worked tirelessly to revive him, applying every advanced life-saving technique in their arsenal, but to no avail. The medical examiner was summoned and the grim task of notifying Trey's mother that he had died would have to fall on some very unfortunate soul. I personally cannot imagine being paid a salary high enough to be the person who makes those calls.

Post-mortem testing of Trey's blood would later reveal a methamphetamine concentration four to five times what would constitute a lethal dose. Friends and family were heartbroken and in a state of disbelief that this twenty-six year-old, bursting at the seams with life, was no longer with us. His body was cremated. Another young, beautiful soul who could have changed the world—reduced to ashes in a vase on his mother's mantle, just two months shy of what would have been his twenty-seventh birthday.

I traveled to Seattle in 2018 to spend that day with Trey's mother, Lara. We laughed a little, cried a lot, and had dinner with one of Trey's best friends from childhood. Lara is a strong woman whose faith in Jesus gets her through the most difficult days. Ever since her precious son passed, she's been "waiting for something beautiful to bloom from all of this." The following is a letter I asked her to write to him that echoes the pain of thousands of parents who have lost their beloved children to this epidemic.

A Mom's Broken Heart: Lara's Letter (Trey's mom) (Washington)

Dear Trey,

I am writing this letter to you knowing you will never read it. My heart aches on a daily basis missing you. Wondering what if…

What if… you were still alive, and we could discuss world politics or the latest song lyrics by your favorite group.

What if… What if I would have known that you were putting on a brave face and that inside you were hurting and scared of failure.

What if… you were still alive, and I could hear your laughter across the room. I would hug you so hard. We would take the trip to the ocean and walk on the beach. You would tell me stories from your time in Cali. The good stuff and the bad stuff.

So many more what ifs…

I was so proud of you for staying clean and sober and for getting a job. You had a 4-year plan and wanted to get back to college. You made some rotten choices. I forgive you. I made some rotten choices and I would ask you to forgive me. I really wanted you to experience the freedom from drugs and from the bondage that drugs entangled you in. I wanted you to see yourself as successful and strong.

Even with the drug addiction you were one of the most resilient people I have ever known. You survived in a dangerous and sketchy place, lived with drug dealers and lived on the street. But you had standards and I think anyone that got to know you when you were sober would realize that you were different.

God gave you so much, a brilliant mind, beautiful heart and a Texas-sized smile. I would be amiss not to mention that you also could be a brat and at times would manipulate me to get your way.

Do you remember when you were a little boy you used to pray for people? You had such a sweet faith. You couldn't wait to get baptized. But life happens and your dad and I divorced, and your life was permanently altered.

What I choose to say to you right now is I LOVE YOU SO MUCH. I miss our long walks staring at the stars and the moon. I miss trips for coffee and shopping.

I miss you Trey and someday I hope to hug you so hard. I love you to the moon and back.

Love,
Mom

Please remember to keep Lara, Elise, Rachel, Aubrey, and countless others whose pain we can only imagine, in your prayers. Their stories are all too common. Their losses are immeasurable. Their pain is forever. I'm eternally grateful to all of these amazing people for allowing me to share their stories so that others might never experience the suffering they've endured. May God bless you all!

CHAPTER 7

Effective Strategies Amidst a Sea of Failures

We are running out of time to find viable, effective solutions to this problem that is crippling us as a nation. Past mistakes have taught us that we're not improving outcomes by throwing exorbitant sums of taxpayer money into draconian policies that mandate stiff penalties and use fear tactics that have proven themselves to be useless as deterrents. So how do we proceed with a plan that will pull us out of this nosedive of addiction?

Our determination and commitment to ending this crisis must be unyielding and approached more vigorously than those who were behind the social engineering campaigns that got us here in the first place. We must resign ourselves to the fact that the task of reversing the damage of the last fifty years will be monumental but is absolutely imperative to save our dying civilization. A major hurdle that must be overcome is the fact that there are many different kinds of people, all in different stages of addiction, with different cultural and religious views and in different age groups, all of whom have different reasons for using drugs, and therefore, all have different needs. There is no single, "one size fits all" solution, and reaching everyone with the message that's right for them will be a challenge.

Obviously the seventeen year-old male who injects heroin daily requires a different approach than the 13 year-old girl who's thinking about trying marijuana for the first time or the gay college sophomore who has just been introduced to crystal meth. The forty-two year-old housewife who takes Percocet for chronic pain also has her own specific set of circumstances and risk factors. There's an important message, however, for everyone in the United States. All must understand the essence of the first four chapters of this book. All must be aware that this epidemic is only a small part of a strategic attack against America.

So many people have been intentionally misled to believe that drugs offer the perfect escape from pain, that they are the best way to show rebellion against authority, or that they're a necessary and deserved part of rewarding oneself for a hard day's work. The reality is, of course, that drug addiction will cause you more pain than it will ever relieve. Although the promotion of drugs in pop culture and music during the 1960s and 1970s may have marked the beginning of this destructive era, the explosion of drug-glorifying themes in today's rap and alternative music have allowed it to flourish. Since the dawn of raves and circuit parties in the late 1980s and early 1990s, an entire subculture has evolved around MDMA (ecstasy). The drugs are getting stronger and those who are addicted are getting younger—in many cases so young that they're incapable of understanding the gravity of the predicament they're putting themselves in.

I've spent much of my adult life working in the trenches as a counselor in one of southern California's busiest acute-care inpatient psychiatric facilities. I worked primarily with teenagers and young adults but have experience with all age groups and patient populations including those with dual diagnoses. I've seen the despair of those who find themselves entangled in this epidemic. I've heard all the excuses. I've seen the best and the worst of those who have championed over and those who have been defeated by the disease of addiction. I've taught. I've listened. I've learned. I've enjoyed the rewarding experiences of helping individual people to get better, all the while watching society as a whole get sicker and sicker. I care. I know what works and what doesn't.

We must ask, specifically, Which components of traditional education and prevention strategies have failed and should therefore be scrapped? What, if anything, has proven to be effective and is, therefore, worth keeping? Should we develop entirely new approaches that don't utilize concepts of the blunders of the past? To date, education and prevention efforts have typically fallen into one of two categories: the repression/abstinence model (RA) and the harm reduction model (HR).[122]

Since the 1980s, programs like D.A.R.E. have targeted millions of children and adolescents with the RA method. The dominating messages generally amount to scare tactics, like the programs led by police officers--elaborate presentations that promise drug use will turn you into a glassy-eyed zombie, cause you to fail at everything in life, and take you down a path that leads straight to jail. At the end students were asked to make a lifelong pledge to never, ever use drugs.[123]

Despite the truest of intentions, there are many problems with this approach. When students are promised that drugs will ruin their lives, only to see peers using drugs who are popular, good athletes, getting accepted to college, and respected by teachers, coaches, and community leaders, much of what they've learned in these programs quickly loses credibility. Such programs are also criticized for being overly-simplistic in nature considering the highly complex series of decisions a teen makes about whether to use drugs or not. Furthermore, these programs lack basic practicality and force commitments that are generally unrealistic. Although programs like D.A.R.E. lost massive funding after being deemed ineffective, the federal government still provides millions of dollars in grants every year to fund programs that continue to push fear-based rhetoric onto high risk youth. It's a recipe for disaster.

More recently, efforts have shifted from abstinence to evidence-based harm reduction. This model accepts the possibility that some students are going to choose to use drugs and shifts the focus to providing factual information to help the teen make safer, more informed choices. Although professionals who are experimenting with this approach claim that their efforts are more effective than traditional models, most haven't been around long enough to yield reliable data that there are any long-term benefits. While harm reduction programs tend to be more interactive than instructional, which is also believed to be a factor associated with better outcomes, this approach has one glaring fundamental problem. It essentially gives students a "green light" to use drugs!

We've spent years telling kids, "Don't use drugs or terrible things will happen to you." Now we're replacing that message with, "Well, okay, since we can't stop you, you might as well do it responsibly." Liberalism in all of its overly permissive glory tends to gloss over the fact that these programs not only condone drug use, but literally provide children and teens with detailed instructions about how to go about it. What an enormous opportunity for grandstanding in the classroom, and for seed-planting in the minds of kids who have no inclination to experiment with drugs. Without a doubt, they come out of programs like this with their interests piqued.

The idea of mature, fact-based discussions sounds appealing to many people, as do programs to encourage simply delaying drug use until adulthood to prevent potential damage to the teen's developing brain, but sending kids any message that it's okay to use illicit drugs, regardless of the context, is just plain *wrong!* It's as wrong as the "Drug Ed." programs the change agents tried to push through Charlotte

Iserbyt's community in the 1970s, and as wrong as the Tavistock Institute's brainwashing techniques that set the stage for the drug culture in the first place. We simply won't solve these problems by capitulating.

I predict that several years from now we're likely to discover that the people who developed this new philosophy that's sweeping the nation will be from the same camp as those who have been pushing for drug-legalization and trying to poison our youth for decades. Remember, the elites still enjoy enormous control over academia, the press, and broadcast media. They dictate their wishes regarding curriculum changes. They decide which research topics get funded and published. They decree which policies are put into place. The propaganda they unleash on the public influences the national conversation, and thereby, the prevailing attitudes of the day. If you think those who profit from the drug trade aren't still highly motivated to create the next generation of new customers, or if you don't believe they have all the tools of societal influence they need to accomplish that goal, you are hereby directed to go back and start reading again, from Chapter 1.

While harm reduction education is inappropriate for naïve or inexperienced children and adolescents, it may have its place with adults who are already addicted. As a conservative, I tend to cringe at the suggestion of taxpayer-funded needle exchange programs and supervised injection centers, but again, solving such a pervasive problem might require many of us to set aside old prejudices, open our minds, and consider experimenting with the handful of solutions that have shown promise in other societies. Whether we like it or not, middle class America no longer has the luxury of viewing this as someone else's problem.

I'm reminded of the scene in the movie, Flight, when Southjet airlines flight 227, piloted by Whip Whitacre (Denzel Washington), experiences mechanical failures that send the aircraft plummeting toward the earth in an uncontrolled dive. As the plane, carrying 127 people, rapidly approaches the ground and the manual controls don't allow the crew to regain control, the pilot decides to execute a bold, radical move to save his passengers, his crew, and himself. Although his co-pilot scoffs at the idea of using what little time they have left to invert the plane, he justifies it stating, "We've gotta do something to stop this dive." The point? If the path you're on leads to imminent disaster, the only solution might seem counterintuitive, or even crazy, but when all else fails, your only option is to change your trajectory any way you possibly can.

A closer look at the harm reduction approach takes us to Portugal, one of the oldest countries on earth, a nation rich with history and culture, that found itself at the height of an opiate crisis in 2001. The country was in the process of total societal breakdown caused by massive overdose deaths, soaring rates of HIV and hepatitis infections, overcrowded jails and prisons, and record high crime rates. Sound familiar? Drugs are still illegal in Portugal, but their government decriminalized possession of small quantities for personal use.[124] California passed similar legislation in 2017,[125] but Portugal took it a step further.

Although they continue to prosecute drug dealers and traffickers, users are now viewed through the lens of public health rather than criminal justice. They receive clean needles, supervised injections, and more importantly, access to rehabilitative services. The results were overwhelmingly positive, as overdose death rates plummeted, along with a reduction in new cases of HIV and other diseases. Crime rates fell to pre-epidemic levels while many addicts found their way into treatment and recovery programs. The net result has been a safer, healthier society, less drug use overall, and dramatically fewer deaths from a wide variety of causes.126 Another program that offered very similar types of services in Vancouver, BC called INSITE also yielded the same types of positive results.127

I live in downtown San Diego, California. When I came to this city 27 years ago, the streets were squeaky clean. Things are different now. Joining the ranks of California's other big cities, we are in the throes of a homeless crisis. Unfortunately, drugs and homelessness often go hand in hand. In the tent communities that now line the streets of what were once immaculate neighborhoods it's not at all uncommon to see used hypodermic needles on public sidewalks. Walk through our streets and eventually you'll see addicts injecting drugs in plain view. Granted, our plight is not as widespread as it is in Los Angeles and San Francisco, but it's nonetheless troubling. People who are justified in worrying that decriminalization will send the wrong messages to young people might weigh their concerns against how children are affected when they see this behavior openly displayed in the clear light of day as they walk or ride the bus to school.

These problems are everywhere, and they're getting worse. As a proud citizen who loves my city, I would welcome a community establishment where adult addicts could go, get help, and if they must engage in this behavior, do so in a private setting without creating a public spectacle. Without any disrespect intended toward those who are addicted and hurting, it's totally unacceptable for our children to have to see this. It could be argued that part of the reason kids start using drugs is due, in part, to the fact that we, as a society, fail to put enough distance between them and adult problems.

Perhaps we should consider launching pilot programs in select cities that provide these opportunities, carefully study the results, and determine if there's any improvement. As the problem reaches further and the death tolls rise, we must remain open to alternative approaches and be willing to consider anything short of legalizing drugs altogether, which would be reckless, irresponsible, and a sure path to our downfall. Fortunately, we live in a society that doesn't limit our ability to change the rules when we need to, to create laws that fix problems and repeal the ones that are creating problems.

A 2014 meta-analysis reviewed the efficacy of 170 traditional school-based drug education and prevention programs. The study found that there have been very few, if any programs that have delivered their intended results. In fact, the overwhelming majority demonstrated no statistically significant effects on long-term abstinence. There are, however, a few strategies within those programs that were identified as being associated with slightly better outcomes, most of which are intuitive. For example, interactive programs in which students engage with educators and peer groups seem slightly more effective, as do those that focus on one drug at a time as opposed to lumping all drugs together. It's also important to match students with material that's age appropriate. Naturally, a program's success also tends to be related to how thoroughly the teachers who facilitate it are trained.[128]

Despite identifying a few aspects of some programs that may or may not be responsible for negligible improvements, their thorough review led the authors to make the following pragmatic statement in their conclusions: "Since the effects of school-based programs are small, they should form part of more comprehensive strategies for drug use prevention in order to achieve a population-level impact."129   In other words, they're not doing enough and need to be supplemented with additional efforts. But perhaps they've overlooked another important possibility. Maybe these programs are, in fact, doing *too* much. Maybe it's time to abandon the idea of pouring resources into programs that we were sold on the idea of by globalist change agents in the first place. In Chapter 9 we return to the topic of drug education and prevention programs and whether they should continue to have a place in our public schools.

The twelve-step approach to recovery that is central to Alcoholics Anonymous (AA), Narcotics Anonymous (NA), etc. deserves a great deal of credit for the simple principles that empower alcoholics and addicts to pull themselves out of patterns of addiction. I've seen it work miracles in the lives of many patients I worked with over the years. For people who believe in it and stick with it, it seems to be a perfect match. Many are able to succeed without needing anything else and insist that they owe their lives to the fellowship of groups like AA and NA.

Twelve-step recovery programs have been successful largely because they accept everyone without judgment, can be found practically anywhere, and access to them is absolutely free. The founders also had great ideas with regard to sponsorship of new attendees, which is basically established program friends in the community making themselves available to newcomers and mentoring them as needed to support their sobriety—in other words, practicing the level of kindness we should all be engaged in within our communities. Since the first A.A. meeting was held in 1935 in Akron, Ohio, millions of men and women whose lives once seemed hopeless have found the way to productive, fulfilling, sober lives through twelve-step programs. Make no mistake, however, they're not for everyone.

Some of the fundamental concepts of A.A. and N.A. are based on assumptions that not everyone can immediately embrace. "Surrendering to a higher power," for example, was a point of contention for many of the teens I worked with, some of whom were still grappling with belief in God. Granted, the program's dogma holds that a higher power can be anything one can surrender to, but some teens, atheists, and others who either have no chosen faith or are struggling with issues of faith may have difficulty internalizing this important theme that's at the heart of the program. The fact that it lacks credentialed professionals is a further limitation in that it can deliver very little to someone who's detoxing or experiencing painful or even life-threatening withdrawals. In some areas, meetings are held in hospitals and other institutions to bring the program to those who can't access them in the community while doctors and nurses manage their medical conditions.

Critics are also quick to attack the twelve-step program's rigid position that addiction is a lifelong disease for which there is no cure and their strict view that any deviation from total abstinence constitutes a "relapse." The fact that it appears to replace one addiction (alcohol/drugs) with another (going to meetings) is another argument some make against twelve-step recovery—a position that's relatively easy to overcome considering the dangers of the former weighed against the benefits of the latter. The warm, accepting nature of these programs coupled with the fact that most of their concepts are simple and relatively easy for newcomers to understand, however, makes them attractive to a lot of people. Once members begin to progress through the textbook, however, and embark on the tasks required to "work the steps," they discover that there's actually a tremendous amount of work involved. People who are less than industrious in their step work are sometimes labeled as lazy or accused of not being fully invested in recovery.

Interestingly, the twelve-step method seems to be the preferred choice of criminal courts and probation officers around the U.S. for defendants charged with drug and alcohol-related crimes as alternatives to custody. Almost all now require completion of accredited inpatient or outpatient programs and proof of attendance at a minimum number of A.A. or N.A. meetings. For several decades, participation in twelve-step programs has also been upheld by psychiatrists and psychologists who care for patients with substance abuse issues, as most recommend it as a part of any long-term treatment plan.

In recent years, the pharmaceutical industry has developed some effective drugs to treat those who are already addicted to opiates. The emergency drug naloxone has saved countless lives and is now saving more than ever before due to increased availability which allows people to keep it at home and administer it to overdose victims. Some addicts have been successfully treated with methadone substitution and more recently suboxone therapy which is prescribed to reduce the agonizing withdrawal symptoms that occur when heroin or other opiate drugs are terminated suddenly.[130] Of course, these drugs are more effective when coupled with psychotherapy as part of a comprehensive treatment plan.

More recent research efforts have been focused on the development of pharmaceutical agents that block the effects of opiates, thereby eliminating the pleasure felt during an opiate "high," and effectively diminishing the motivation to use. Another promising pharmacological approach involves the buprenorphine-naloxone complex. These drugs provide an opiate (buprenorphine) to relieve withdrawal symptoms and an opioid agonist (naloxone), which blocks opiate receptors, thereby preventing the euphoric feeling that opiate addicts chase. A major obstacle that stands between these drugs and the public, however, is the fact that only one out of every eight physicians holds the specialized credentials needed to prescribe them.[131]

Everyone in America must be encouraged to consider the specific roles they play in perpetuating this enormous social problem. Parents must be taught effective ways to talk with their kids about drugs. It's also important that they're able to take an honest and accurate assessment of themselves and the examples they set via their own behaviors. Parents with substance abuse issues who may need assistance must have such resources available to them through private sector and community-based organizations. If we've learned anything from our failures, we know that people's deep seated personal problems are not typically solved by the heavy hand of big government weighing down on them.

Medical students must receive mandatory training about the importance of prescribing pain medications responsibly. Practicing physicians must be required to complete continuing education units that keep them informed about these issues in a constantly changing world. Pressure must be exerted on the media to provide content that's honest and socially responsible. It's not enough for one of these conditions to be satisfied. We must strive as a nation to meet all of them, and a good place to start these conversations involves simply informing people that we're the victims of a war that's being waged by forces that are wholly committed to our destruction. Everyone must understand that we're being programmed to destroy ourselves, and that fighting back is our only path to salvation. The next chapter offers some suggestions about how to approach these topics with young people.

The attempted shift to world governance has been in progress longer than most of us have been alive. Those who perpetuate it aren't likely to surrender any time soon. We can give the next generation of Americans an advantage that we didn't have, as most of us were oblivious to the globalists' agenda until the internet improved our ability to share this information on a larger scale. We can no longer afford to be silent, passive, or complacent. We must spread the word and become the resistance. Please, educate your kids. Educate everyone in your circles of influence, not just about drugs, but also about the looming, omnipresent threat of globalism, the power of social engineering, and the diabolical will of the elites.

The purpose of the next chapter is to convey an important and truthful message to young people—a series of bold, factual statements that are intended to establish or change their beliefs about why drugs are pushed in our society, how they're intended to be roadblocks that separate people from their dreams, and how to defeat the enemy by staying on the winning team. It also provides some expert tips for parents about how to engage in meaningful and effective discussions about these topics with their kids.

CHAPTER 8

The Life You Deserve:
An Urgent Message to Young People

You have a decision to make. It doesn't have to be a tough decision, but it's a big decision. Your parents and teachers can guide you. Your friends can tell you what they think is right for you. TV shows, song lyrics, and people on social media can also try to influence your thoughts. But the choices you make about whether drugs will or will not be a part of your future are yours to make, and yours alone. We make our best decisions when we have as much information as possible. Your life and your future matter, so you deserve to know as much as you possibly can when you're confronted with choices that will determine your life's path.

The world is full of many different kinds of people. There are those who care about others and want life to be better for everyone. Then, there are also those who do not. The people we follow and listen to shape our view of the world and the things we grow up thinking are important. We want you to be successful. We want all your dreams to come true. Most of all, we want you to be happy. Some of the most powerful people in the world, however, want something very different for you. This is not to say that they have anything against you personally. In fact, they most likely have no idea who you are. They want you to fail simply because you're an American. Their goal is to destroy our country by destroying our population, and they've got the money and the power to make it happen.

You've probably been told how lucky you are to live in a country where freedom provides endless opportunities. That's all true. But, unfortunately, there are people who want to take those opportunities away from us, and they've been trying to accomplish this for a very long time. They want the American people to be poor, weak, and most of all, unable to fight back. They figured out that one of the ways they could hurt our country the most would be to get as many people as possible addicted to drugs. If you look around at our society, you'll see that their plan is going well.

You might know someone who is addicted to drugs, or perhaps even someone who has died from a habit that went outside of their control, but a tragic story like this doesn't have to be your life. You have a chance to fight back. At this point, you might not care about your country, your fellow citizens, or the future of humanity. You might not be concerned about broad trends in society that involve a lot of people you've never met. But you probably care about what happens to you and your friends and family, and that's why you should listen very carefully to the rest of what we have to say.

You've probably gotten a lot of mixed messages about drugs. For example, you've probably learned about drugs in school, where you were told about risks of overdose, consequences of drinking and driving, and the negative impact drugs can have on your health. You may have friends who use drugs, and what they're telling you might seem to contradict all of that. As if that wasn't confusing enough, you've seen TV shows, listened to music, and gone to movies that told you drugs will make you more attractive, more interesting, and more popular. So, is anybody actually telling you the truth? If you're wondering why all of this information doesn't add up, trust me, you're not alone! We respect you, and we want to help you figure it all out so you can decide what's best for you.

Before we get into that, though, let's take a moment to talk about competition. Depending on how driven we are, life seems to be an endless series of races, contests, and other situations that require us to prove ourselves. When we're young, we compete in sports and athletics, we compete in academics, and we compete for popularity and attention and recognition from our peers. Most of us try to minimize our flaws, enhance our talents, and work hard to become better, smarter, stronger, and faster than we were yesterday. There's no better feeling than scoring the winning point for your team, getting the highest grade in the class, or being voted by your peers as being the best at something. But not everyone can be number one. Not everyone can get into the best college. Not everyone can be the best singer, dancer, or athlete. We compete for these things and, as you know, the more people there are to compete with, the harder you have to work to be the best. I wish I could tell you that competitions magically stop when you turn 18 or attend your last day of high school, but they don't.

We enter the adult world only to find that we're forced to compete more than we've ever had to before, and it's all complicated by the fact that we're up against people we don't know. You might compete with hundreds of other people for a job you want. Some applicants won't be qualified at all. Some will be less qualified than you. Some might be more qualified, but one thing is certain. Only one person will get the job.

Whether we're trying to get a job, get a date, get a loan, or get anything that requires us to compete with others for what we want, it helps to have as many advantages as we possibly can, and making the most of the resources we have is key to getting rewarded in life. Of course, being kind, caring about others, and generally being a good person are rewarding on another level, but putting our best foot forward also makes us even more effective at doing those things. We make the most of the talents, abilities, and advantages we have in life while struggling to overcome our disadvantages, limitations, and challenges. One of the hardest things we encounter is having to accept our limitations, but we all have them, and the fewer we start out with, and the more we can do to overcome them, the better the chance we have of making our dreams become reality.

So, what does any of this have to do with using drugs? This is where the impact of the choice that only you can make comes in. You have to ask yourself, "What advantages do I have right now? What do I have that will help me to compete with the growing number of people who all want the same things I want? What are my limitations and how can I overcome them?" Pay particular attention to following statement because it's the "take home" message. Despite any misinformation you may have received up to this point, let's be very clear:

Using drugs *will* limit your abilities, take away your advantages and make it more difficult for you to compete in life for the things you want.

Before getting into the reasons why this is true, read that statement again. Read it to yourself, then read it out loud so you hear yourself say it. Now consider the people who want to destroy the people of our country. They want to take away our advantages. They want to limit our success. They want us to be unable to compete. Now ask yourself if you need some extra limitations in your life. Can you afford to risk losing the advantages you have? This is the logic that you need to apply to these decisions, because it's the most practical way of looking at it.

Drugs will limit you. We know that when people start using drugs, they stop doing other things that they used to enjoy. They also tend to abandon their old friends and family and start hanging out with other people who use because they feel accepted among them because they don't have to face the social consequences of their actions. Eventually they withdraw from activities until they've dropped out of society completely. They become irresponsible and lose interest in taking care of themselves. They lose jobs and miss their biggest opportunities. Their relationships with friends and family begin to deteriorate. Their lives become all about losses, so they dive deeper into using drugs as a way to escape. Eventually the drugs are all they have left. They stop caring about their health or appearance. What seemed like a way to have more friends and more energy when they started has left them sick, exhausted, broke, alone, and miserable. This becomes the story of everyone who chooses the path of drugs regardless of the advantages they might have started out with. So why do so many people do it?

Nobody wakes up one morning and says to themselves, "I really want to become a drug addict." There are no college courses that teach young people who dream everything they need to know about destroying their lives with addiction. Nobody intends to get addicted. People don't expect drugs to take control of them and turn their lives upside down, but the process of becoming addicted can happen very quickly.

While it's happening the person is not able to see or admit it. Once addicted, they tend to blame others for the problems drugs are causing in their lives, and often make excuses for themselves and their behavior. They'll slowly let go of everything that ever mattered to them, all the while desperately clinging to the one thing that caused the losses in the first place—the drugs.

Some of the movies, the music kids listen to, and some TV shows paint a very unrealistic picture of what drugs do to people. They may depict them as strong, beautiful, carefree, and successful—driving nice cars, wearing expensive clothes, surrounded by good-looking friends. All of this is put out there by people who want to deceive you. They want you to see this and think, "that's what I want," but they don't tell you that using drugs is the best way to make sure you never have any of those things. They don't show you the pain, the suffering, or the real consequences that are inevitable when you trade in your dreams for a drug habit.

Earlier we discussed how difficult it is to make it in today's world where there are so many people all competing for the same resources. Ask yourself why you would want to burden yourself with more limitations that make it even harder to survive? Do you want to surrender to the people who lie to you and try to seduce you with drugs so that you'll fail at achieving your dreams and die young?

You have to be wise in every decision you make. If you don't think drugs can ruin your life, look around and take note of the problems they've created in our society at large. They've brought crime and violence to our communities. They've ripped families apart and made successful people go bankrupt. And yes, they've taken hundreds of thousands of innocent young people who once had bright futures ahead of them out of our communities and put them in jails, hospitals, and cemeteries. If you want a shot at being happy, if you want a chance to have all the things in life you deserve, you need to avoid the chaos and destruction drugs bring to the lives of those who invite them in.

There's an attack being launched against your generation. You have the chance to be so much smarter than the generations that came before you. We hope you will fight back, tell your friends, and send the evil people who want to ruin your life a loud and clear message, "Thanks, but no thanks!" Protect your body, protect your mind, and protect your relationships with your family and your real friends. You'll need all of them to succeed in life. There are endless ways to have fun that will open doors for you instead of robbing you of your health, talents, and opportunities. One by one, drugs will slam all of those doors shut. Don't take our word for it. Look around. Pay close attention to other kids and adults around you. Ask questions and start planning how you're going to get what you want in life. Don't let *anyone* talk you out of it! Take care and good luck to you!

A Parent's Guide: Talking to Your Kids About Drugs

It's important for parents to remember that the decision a child makes to use drugs or not to use drugs will be theirs and theirs alone. Chances are, you won't be there to guide them in those critical moments, but there is much you can do to prepare children and give them the power and confidence that will help them to make the right decisions. The following is a list of suggestions from notable psychologists and other professionals about how to approach and discuss substance abuse with kids of all ages. According to the experts, there are right and wrong ways to engage in these conversations. We offer some "dos" and "don'ts" as shared by some of the brightest minds of our time.

❖ **Start Early**

You'll want to be ahead of the game and talk to your kids before they've been offered a chance to try drugs for the first time. Some experts recommend beginning discussions when children are between the ages of 8 and 10 years old. Others suggest that preliminary discussions should begin as early as pre-school, which may include explaining to them that medications are very powerful and why they must be handled with care. Otherwise they can make them very sick or even be life-threatening. These are concepts that even very young children are able to grasp.

Keep the conversations age-appropriate and avoid overwhelming your kids with too much information at once. It's imperative that you do not wait until your child is in high school to start having these talks. It's much better for them to get the facts from you before they begin to hear the misinformation spread by their peers.

❖ **Make it about health, not fear.**

Avoid fear-mongering and scare tactics. Stay away from emotionally charged discussions and harsh statements of condemnation or judgment, which are guaranteed ways to lose their attention and make them reluctant to come to you when they feel pressured or need advice. Traditional "scared-straight" methods have been proven ineffective at best and are most likely counterproductive. Instead, clarify what your values are as they relate to good health and smart choices. Explain the health consequences of using drugs in the context of letting them know that you want them to have long and healthy lives.

❖ **Discuss. Don't lecture. Keep it in the present.**

When kids, especially teenagers, feel they're being lectured, their initial reaction is often to tune out or shut down. Talk *with* them instead of to them. Make them an active part of a two-way dialogue. Encourage them to share their thoughts, ask questions, and let them know you respect their opinions even if they need to be redirected. It's also a good idea to practice/role-play different situations and help them come up with ways they can respond if and when they find themselves under pressure to make a decision.

Kids of all ages tend to focus on what's going on here and now. They should be encouraged to think about the future and to process how the decisions they make today will affect their futures, but since kids have trouble connecting to hypothetical events in the distant future, it's hard to motivate them by pointing out potential long-term consequences. This makes it more practical to focus primarily on more immediate, short-term conditions. For example, a parent might tell the teenager that if he or she uses drugs, the privilege of driving will be taken away or some other type of immediate restriction will be imposed. The older they get, the more capable they should be of relating to the future and long-term consequences.

❖ **Be honest. Be a living example.**

This is especially true when your kids ask you about your own experiences with substance use/abuse. While you don't want to discuss your own past in a way that glamorizes drug use or reinforces a their possibility of thinking, "See, you did it and you turned out alright," remember that kids can often tell when we're not being truthful. Some may have already heard about things you've done in the past from other family members, etc. If they should find out at some point in the future that you weren't honest with them, it could destroy your credibility in these discussions which may, in their minds, justify disobeying you.

Rather than feeling the need to avoid the question entirely or lie through your teeth, you can use it as an opportunity to say something like, "I've made some mistakes in my time," or "I might have been better off if I would have…" Kids will appreciate the honesty and a little self-disclosure can go a long way in terms of establishing the level of trust you'll want them to feel when they have more questions. You'd much rather have them coming to you for advice than going to one of their peers or grappling with tough decisions on their own.

Set an appropriate example. Kids are very quick to note hypocrisy and aren't big fans of "Do as I say, not as I do." Remember that your behaviors are being closely studied, even when you might not realize it. If they see you drinking excessively to celebrate some good news or to dull the pain of a bad experience, they're naturally going to think those responses are normal and acceptable.

❖ **Make it an ongoing, fact-based discussion.**

Don't wait until the night of the big party to start talking about these issues, which could be perceived as a lack of trust or an effort to control them or ruin their fun. Take advantage of opportunities that come up (e.g., after a movie that touches on the subject, or upon seeing an ad or driving by a billboard) to open a conversation that shares what your values are and lets you assess their level of understanding.

It's natural for parents to want to avoid or delay these discussions. It's much easier to tell ourselves everything is okay and not talk about it unless a problem arises. But it's important to address these topics in a way that relates to the child's reality and not the world we wished they lived in. Also, be careful not to fall into the trap of believing that once you've had a discussion, no matter how successful it might have seemed, that your job is done. You'll want to check in with them regularly to see what's changed, what new pressures they may have experienced since the last conversation, and how they handled it. This doesn't mean having a formal meeting at the same time every week, but bringing it up from time to time, and taking advantage of the thousands of opportunities that naturally present themselves will help to make sure you're both on the same page even as their situations change.

❖ **Don't dole out drugs at home.**

The examples you set at home are powerful. Avoid making statements like, 'Oh, you have a headache? I have some leftover Vicodin here somewhere." This not only sends the message that prescription drugs are safe to be passed around freely, but also undermines respect for the laws that govern controlled substances, which are in place to protect consumers. Discard your unused medications so they aren't sitting around in medicine cabinets where they can become potential temptations.

If they are prescribed pain medications, make sure you administer them on the right schedule. Don't ever turn them loose with a bottle of opiates which may create a tough situation with their peers who may try to manipulate them into selling them or giving them away. If you monitor what they're taking, it will send them a strong message: that irresponsible handling of drugs can lead to very negative consequences. You want them to understand that drugs can offer tremendous, even life-saving benefits when used properly, but can be extremely dangerous when abused.

❖ **Be kind but be firm.**

Although most children and teenagers will tell you exactly the opposite, they're happiest and feel most secure when we set firm boundaries for them. Tell them in clear, direct terms exactly what is and what is not acceptable behavior, then stick to your guns. Although you are the authority figure, you're asking them to make adult decisions, so speak to them in a way that shows you recognize their maturity and individuality. They're most likely going to remember your words in the moments they're confronted with tough decisions. Having mature conversations now will be more likely to result in mature decisions being made when it matters most.

❖ **Network with other concerned parents.**

You're not in this alone. Your kids may try to tell you that "so and so's parents let them…" but don't fall for it. Most parents have the same concerns about their kids that you have. Family dynamics and work schedules might make them unable to provide supervision at all times. Help each other out. Share information. Reciprocate good communication. Be each other's eyes and ears. Talk to them about how you've talked to your kids about drugs and ask them how they've talked to theirs.

You can learn so much from each other. You never know what senseless tragedy could be prevented if parents weren't afraid to speak up when they see something unusual. You're all in this together and other parents might have important information about something your child hasn't shared with you. Support each other and stay in touch in the interest of healthier kids and a safer community.

CHAPTER 9

Recovering Together as a Nation

How do we recover from this national crisis that has taken generations to escalate to the level we're experiencing today? When considering the reasons so many efforts to address the problem has failed, we must remember that many of those attempts have been half-hearted at best. We shouldn't expect effective solutions to be proposed by those who stand to benefit most from the status quo—the same reason we wouldn't consult an arsonist for fire safety tips. The answers are not likely to come from an overinflated, bureaucratic government which, as we've demonstrated throughout this book, has been corrupted to its core by greed, lust for power, and those who have joined in the quest for world government. This is a problem of the people and must be solved for the people and by the people.

Our efforts should include a defensive strategy, the goals of which must be tailored to address the needs of different groups in society: those who have had no exposure to drugs who are potential victims of this war against humanity, those who are already using but continue to function in society, and those whose lives have already been consumed by the addiction process. We must also address the large number of people who are currently incarcerated and those from disadvantaged backgrounds who see the drug trade as their only path to economic opportunity. We are all victims, or potential victims, as the elites' plan is aimed at destroying all of us indiscriminately. Defending ourselves and our fellow citizens must become reflexive.

We must also develop an offensive strategy that focuses on defeating those who have deliberately inflicted this suffering upon us. We must target them and render them incapable of future attacks against our culture. Our responses, both offensive and defensive must be far more aggressive, more determined, and more organized than the aggressors' acts against us have been. Although their surprise attack may have weakened us, they have by no means defeated us. Instead, they've disturbed a sleeping giant who is now wide awake and ready to go after them.

The following list reviews some key points we've established as facts in the previous chapters, each of which should be considered independently and as part of a larger picture.

❖ The drug crisis that is crippling our nation is the result of an orchestrated plan developed by the elites and their social engineers to destroy our culture.

❖ The illicit drug trade is a trillion dollar per year industry that lubricates the world economy.

❖ Powerful positions in governments, corporations, and various institutions have been infiltrated and hijacked by operatives who keep this destructive cycle perpetually in motion.

❖ The news, entertainment, and broadcast media have also been taken over and are not only complicit in but have become an integral part of this finely tuned machine of destruction.

❖ The war on drugs, despite hundreds of billions of taxpayer dollars spent and countess human resources utilized over a fifty year period, has not only failed to produce any significant reduction in drug use, but has also created a litany of social woes including mass incarceration, increases in violent crime rates, dissolution of families, and empowerment of corrupt forces around the globe.

- ❖ We are currently in a rare and advantageous position under the administration of President Trump, who is not beholden to the establishment, genuinely cares about the future and welfare of the American people, and is committed to fighting this crisis. We must make the most of this unique opportunity.

- ❖ There are new ideas and policies that are being evaluated in the U.S. and around the world that are showing promise and providing hope that these problems are solvable. We must abandon outdated approaches and align our efforts with newer models that have demonstrated the potential to be effective.

I am only one man. My ability to make a difference in this crisis is limited by my resources, the length of my reach, and my own personal set of God-given abilities. Fortunately, we are all blessed with talents that align with our individual callings in life. I'm blessed to have this insight and the gift of words which allows me to enlighten others. In doing so, I hope to penetrate the hearts and minds of those who possess different talents, abilities, and strengths, and that you will put them to work to make a positive difference. The final subsections present some ideas, discuss some important considerations, and offer suggestions for those who are far more brilliant and capable than I, who feel inspired to affect the kind of change that will reverse the downward spiral drugs have dragged our wounded society into. May God bless you, the reader, and may God forever bless the United States of America!

Unite and Conquer

There's no need to mince words. Our nation is fractured. We've been separated and pushed into opposing comers based on political views, race, religion, gender, class, and the list goes on and on. Of course, race-biting and identity politics are as much an integral part of the globalists' social engineering strategy as creation of the drug culture. The concept of "divide and conquer" dates back to Biblical times as an effective strategy for defeating any group of people, whether it be the members of a household or the rulers of an empire.

As Americans, we're constantly bombarded with a frenzy of media-driven propaganda aimed at calling attention to our differences and ramping up powerful emotional responses that draw the lines of separation between "us" and "them." In spite of this, we remain a relatively peaceful nation. So why haven't we taken the bait? Americans have a great deal more in common with one another than the powers that be would like for us to believe. Survey a random sample of 1,000 of us, and you're likely to find that the overwhelming majority of us have very similar core values. We're people who believe in freedom, value fairness, demand justice, embrace tolerance and equality, stand up for sanctity of life, and support the right of all creatures to live with self-determination. These concepts are at the very foundation of who we are. They're woven into the moral fabric of our society regardless of whether we identify as Democrat or Republican, black or white, Christian or Jewish, gay or straight, etc.

We demonstrate our unity whenever our fellow citizens are victims of violent acts or natural disasters that leave people hurting and in need of help. We don't see colors or other lines of division during these defining moments. We race to help other people, dig deeply into our pockets to give, and proudly volunteer our time and energy to relieve the suffering of others because we're people of good will. Despite their best efforts, no one has managed to change that.

When former CIA agent turned whistleblower, Kevin Shipp, was asked what Americans can do to regain control of the rogue forces that exist within our own government, he stated simply, "We've got to stop letting them divide us between liberal vs. conservative and Democrat vs. Republican. We've got to come together as one people, with one unifying goal. That is the only way we can take our power back." Although this statement was made regarding regaining control of the CIA and other powerful government entities, it holds true for practically every problem we face as a nation. The elites have spent billions of dollars promoting chaos and division in the United States and Europe. Indeed, it would be "game over" for them if we were able to somehow overcome our differences and unite in a coalition of defiance. As unlikely as this sounds, remember that the ideas that divide us have been learned. They can absolutely be "unlearned."

When we're all shouting different things at the same time, our voices cannot be heard. When we're all shouting the same thing at the same time, our *voice* cannot be ignored. We grew up with a tradition of reciting some powerful words every morning, "One nation, under God, indivisible, with liberty and justice for all." That familiar, time-honored phrase is key to solving this and other problems that are compounded by the barriers that divide us.

Grassroots "Community Organizing"

President Barack Obama spoke frequently to his followers about "community organizing" as a way to affect social justice. Of course, he borrowed this term from the late Saul Alinsky, a highly controversial writer from the 1960s, best known for his Marxist/Socialist diatribe, *Rules for Radicals*. I'm no fan of Obama or Alinsky, but they both hit the nail on the head with regard to changing the nation through organization of local, grassroots efforts that begin at the community level.

These messages must be spread to every community in America, where it will be up to good people (yes, they exist in every community) to take appropriate action. Ideally, the Christian church should sponsor a network ministry and take on the tasks of community outreach, mentoring, and developing local strategies to step into the lives of children whose families have let them down and adults whose lives have been torn apart by addiction. We must engage with incarcerated men and women who need positive attention and direction while also reaching out to those who are at highest risk of falling victim to perils that await them.

2020 is not the year for Christ's followers to hide behind locked doors in gated communities, isolating ourselves from the evil that exists outside. It's time for us to roll up our sleeves, put ourselves out there, and fight to take back the souls of our communities. We must act as Christ did—with strength, humility, and hearts full of compassion for our fellow citizens who need prayer, guidance, and the only genuine fulfillment that can replace the emptiness they've come to know. It's time for pastors and ministers to call on their congregations—to organize, mobilize, and salvage the hearts and minds of the American people.

> "Each one should use whatever gift he has received to serve others, faithfully administering God's grace in its various forms."
>
> --1 Peter 4:10

Until the citizens of the United States can reclaim control of our schools, utilizing them as sites for drug "education and prevention" is likely to do more harm than good. Not every child has the inclination to use drugs. Programs that teach those kids everything they need to know to become fully functioning addicts are counterproductive at best. We should demand that schools stick to academics, although they can be extremely useful in identifying students with potential problems and discretely referring them, along with their parents, to outside sources of help. Beyond that, their involvement is not only useless, but detrimental to other students.

By no means should this be taken as a suggestion that schools should tolerate drug activity—quite the opposite. Schools must have a tough, "zero-tolerance" stance on drugs. The policy should be, "If you're using or selling drugs or bringing drugs to school, you're out of school, effective immediately, and until a rigorous, approved rehabilitation program clears you to come back, period! No exceptions! No excuses! If you don't complete the program in a timely manner, your parents will be held accountable for truancy." The problem behavior is thereby removed immediately without influencing other students.

If schools are truly doing their jobs, the only appropriate discussion of drugs would be in the academic context of an advanced science course or perhaps as part of legitimate study in the social sciences. Curriculum designed to teach groups of innocent children and adolescents what drugs are, how they make you feel, and how to use them correctly in peer groups where those with experience are likely to grandstand and glamorize the problem behavior is just plain moronic. With foolishness like this going on, is it any wonder we have a raging drug epidemic that's claiming 70,000 American lives every year? It's time to get smart.

God bless the teachers of today. They are the true heroes and warriors of our time. The vast majority, however, are not mental health professionals and lack the expertise to lead curious teens through discussions on the complex issues surrounding substance abuse. They're not trained in this arena, nor should they be expected to fill this role. What an enormous train wreck drug education and prevention programs have been for everyone involved. Enough is enough! It's failed, already!

Education and prevention programs for youth must be left to the mental health professionals who work only with those who demonstrate a need for their services. Unless a problem is detected, schools should presume that parents are doing their jobs, talking to their kids, and teaching them about the dangers of using drugs. Divert all federal funding currently provided for drug education in schools to public education and treatment centers that serve the needs of families who have been referred by the schools for drug problems. Period. End of story!

Economic Concerns: Timing is Everything

Whether we like it or not, it's a reality that profits from drug sales are currently vital to the global economy. Experts agree that any sudden disruption in the flow of dirty drug money would cause the collapse of individual economic markets and potentially trigger a global economic crisis. Like an addict experiencing painful withdrawals, the world must be gradually weaned off of the effects of drug money. I am by no means an expert in economics but propose that the only way to end the illicit drug trade without paralyzing the world economy, sending billions of people who are already struggling straight to the brink of starvation, is to do it slowly. Of course, we can expect accomplishing these changes to take years, if not decades, anyway, but care must be taken to protect innocent people who could be seriously harmed by the economic consequences.

If steps are taken to gradually dry up the enormous market created by the demand for drugs, the largest consumer of course being the United States, while trying to fortify the economies of nations most dependent on profits from drug sales with alternative industries, we could theoretically phase this sector of the economy out without creating a devastating ripple effect across the globe. I readily admit that I have no idea how to accomplish this and yield the complex details to economists who like to be challenged.

Legal Concerns: A Word to Legislators and the Judiciary

As previously stated, a sweeping repeal of legislation that punishes drug offenders would have devastating consequences, both short and long term. Legalizing drugs would, in effect, be viewed as an endorsement of drug use by the government, leading to millions of new addicts hitting the streets, a surge in use among those already addicted leading to an unpredictable number of overdose deaths, and the empowerment of ruthless drug suppliers who would see it as an opportunity for unlimited profits. Lawmakers, judges, and law enforcement, however, are afforded opportunities to exercise discretion at several points throughout the criminal justice process. Although prison sentences do little to rehabilitate inmates, prosecution by the government must always remain as a last resort for those who fail to comply with court-ordered interventions.

To better serve defendants in cases where leniency is not permitted by statute, legislation should be amended to allow judges flexibility and discretion. Prosecutors and judges must view those brought into the criminal justice system for drug offenses, especially for the first time, as opportunities to offer an array of services, the need for which must be tailored to best accommodate the individual and assessed on a case-by-case basis by qualified intake personnel. Many states have already begun to adopt similar policies, but there is no fairness in having to complete a program in California for the same offense that's punishable by a ten year sentence in Alabama. Only in the rarest of circumstances should people be imprisoned for non-violent drug offenses, but they should always live with the knowledge that they could be if the courts deem them as unwilling to participate in the recovery process.

Effort must be made to remove the stigma that prevents many people from seeking help. Grants for treatment programs must be used wisely in that only those with proven track records will be funded and approved by the courts as acceptable, with the greatest emphasis placed on juvenile programs that rehabilitate children and teens using an approach that requires active involvement of parents or guardians. Programs must be supportive and tolerant of those who demonstrate an intertest in sober living and personal responsibility.

We must also, as some states have, avoid branding drug users as criminals for life. Stories are all too common of people who have served their time, paid their debt to society, and are successfully rehabilitated, only to be prevented from fully re-entering society by the existence of ominous criminal records that scar them for life. Privacy laws protect individual medical records such that health issues are kept confidential, but a drug addiction, which is a medical condition by definition, becomes a matter of public record. This is clearly an injustice and a setup for failure that all but guarantees that many people, desperate to survive, will return to previous cycles of criminal behavior unless they are able to leave their past behind them and start anew. Everyone must be given multiple opportunities to redeem themselves without prejudice.

Educating Future Generations

Of course, it's important for parents to talk to their kids about the dangers associated with using drugs, but we can't stop there. It's vitally important that they understand the issue in terms of the globalists' agenda and the push for world government. After all, they're the leaders and warriors of tomorrow. If we arm them with the truth about the elites' attacks against America, they'll be in a much more favorable position to fight back than previous generations have been. Many of us had no idea this sinister plot existed until the internet revolutionized our ability to disseminate information around the globe.

The schools are not going to teach our kids lessons in patriotism and morality or give them access to the true stories of American History. It is therefore up to us to make sure they can identify efforts to destroy our country, our Constitution, and our founding principles. Explain to them the significance of social engineering tactics that we've all been victims of. Give them examples of how the powerful influence of the elites has been working against us for more than a century. Make sure they understand that these threats haven't gone away, nor are they likely to do so anytime soon.

Social Media and "Social Re-engineering"

It has taken many years and a tremendous amount of underhanded trickery to lead us to where we find ourselves today. Anything that can be learned, however, can be unlearned, and in this case, must be unlearned if we are to survive and prosper as we did during the first 150 years of our history. Who's to say we can't beat the elites at their own game? People don't typically welcome those whose intent is to kill them into their lives with open arms. If massive campaigns designed to spread the facts presented in this book can convince all people that drugs are a direct, personal attack against their well-being, then perhaps they will avoid them as an act of self-defense or self-preservation. The possibilities in this realm are endless.

Anything that can be dreamed up by evil people in think tanks on the other side of the Atlantic can be countered by smart, determined people here at home. Who should be making the rules and defining the norms in our society? Should our fate be chosen by a cabal of evil sycophants who regard us as "useless eaters" and the "unbathed masses," or should we be the ones calling the shots? The American people are resourceful, resilient, and creative. Now that it's clear how this happened, I challenge the readers, each of you with your own special talents, gifts, and abilities to think long and hard about how we can "re-engineer" our culture in such a way that the idea of using illicit drugs becomes widely unpopular among young people, among all people.

Granted, it may take some time, but imagine a day when illicit drug markets begin to dry up, shipments to the United States are rejected, and the ruthless, corrupt cartels are sent a loud, clear message, "The U.S. isn't interested in buying your drugs anymore." We're living in a time of amazing opportunity. Social media gives everyday people a platform that allows us to share our ideas with literally billions of people around the globe. It was the game-changer in the 2016 U.S. presidential election. It gives each of us unlimited potential to create lasting changes in our nation and in our world. I've planted the seeds. Now it's up to *you* to make them grow!

1 Arthur Thompson, *To the Victor Go the Myths and Monuments* (Appleton, WI: American Opinions Foundation Publishing, 2018).
2 Jack Eble, "U.S. Army plans recruiting push as number of qualified Americans dwindles," *Fox 43 News*, June 13, 2019. https://www.fox43.com/article/news/local/contests/u-s-army-plans-recruiting-push-as-number-of-qualified-americans-dwindles/521-da1bb406-96c0-4313-951f-f8d29df681e9
3 Holly Hedehaard, "Drug Overdose Deaths in the United States, 1999-2016," N*CHS Data Brief, no. 294*, December 2017. https://www.cdc.gov/nchs/data/databriefs/db294.pdf
4 Ibid.
5 Ibid.
6 Ibid.
7 Julie R. Gaither, "US National Trends in Pediatric Deaths from Prescription and Illicit Opioids," 1999-2016. *Journal of the American Medical Association*, December 28, 2018. https://jamanetwork.com/journals/jamanetworkopen/fullarticle/271958.
8 Nathan Yerby, "Statistics on Addiction in America," *Addiction Center*, December 5, 2019. https://www.addictioncenter.com/addiction/addiction-statistics/
9 Ibid.

10 Mark Edmund Rose, "Are Prescription Opioids Driving the Opioid Crisis? Assumptions vs Facts," *Journal of Pain Medicine*, April 19, 2018. https://www.ncbi.nlm.nih.gov/pmc/articles/PMC6018937/.
11 Adam Warner, "America's Deadly Opioid Epidemic by the Numbers," *NBCNews4*, November 19, 2017. https://www.nbcnewyork.com/news/local/americas-deadly-opioid-epidemic-by-the-numbers/348106/.
12 John Gramlich, "As fatal overdoses rise, many Americans see drug addiction as a major problem in their community," *Factank News in the Numbers*, May 30, 2018. https://www.pewresearch.org/fact-tank/2018/05/30/as-fatal-overdoses-rise-many-americans-see-drug-addiction-as-a-major-problem-in-their-community.
13 Lester Holt, "The Opiate Epidemic," *NBC News*, September 4, 2018. https://www.latest.facebook.com/watch/?v=10155561573258689
14 Ibid.

15 Kristine Philips, "Drugs are killing so many people in Ohio that cold-storage trailers are being used as morgues," *The Washington Post,* March 15, 2017. https://www.washingtonpost.com/news/to-your-health/wp/2017/03/16/drugs-are-killing-so-many-in-this-county-that-cold-storage-trailers-are-being-used-as-morgues/.

16 Eric Eyre, "Drug firm poured 3M opioids into WV town in just 10 months, report says," *Charleston Gazette-Mail,* December 19, 2018. https://www.wvgazettemail.com/news/health/drug-firm-poured-m-opioids-into-wv-town-in-just/article_d229b33b-c55a-5451-ab3f-b545476516d4.html.

17 Kaitlynn LeBeau, "New study calls for more help for drug-addicted babies," *NBC News*, October 5, 2017. https://www.wsaz.com/content/news/New-study-calls-for-more-help-for-drug-addicted-babies-449646293.html.

18 Sara Warfield, "Opioid-Related Outcomes in West Virginia, 2008–2016," American Journal of Public Health, February 2019. https://ajph.aphapublications.org/doi/abs/10.2105/AJPH.2018.304845?journalCode=ajph.

19 Jake Flatley, "West Virginia files suit against opioid maker Purdue Pharma," *Metro News: The Voice of West Virginia*, May 16, 2019. http://wvmetronews.com/2019/05/16/west-virginia-files-suit-against-opioid-maker-purdue-pharma/.

20 Abbey Goodnough, "Drug Overdose Deaths Drop in U.S. for First Time Since 1990," *The New York Times*, July 27, 2019. https://www.nytimes.com/interactive/2019/07/17/upshot/drug-overdose-deaths-fall.html.

21 Ibid.

22 Martha Bebinger, "Seizures of methamphetamine are surging in the U.S.," *MPR News*, July 29, 2019. https://www.mprnews.org/story/2019/07/29/npr-seizures-of-methamphetamine-are-surging-in-the-u-s.

23 Ibid.

24 Mbabazi, Karlisa, "Drug Overdose Deaths Involving Cocaine and Psychostimulants with Abuse Potential — United States, 2003–2017," *Medscape,* May 2019. https://www.medscape.com/viewarticle/912587.

25 Christopher McCall Jones, "Recent Increases in Cocaine-Related Overdose Deaths and the Role of Opioids," *American Journal of Public Health*, March 2017. https://www.ncbi.nlm.nih.gov/pmc/articles/PMC5296707/.

26 NIDA Staff Writer, "What is the scope of marijuana use in the United States?" *National Institute on Drug Abuse*, December 24, 2019.

https://www.drugabuse.gov/publications/research-
reports/marijuana/what-scope-marijuana-use-in-united-states.
27 Ibid.
28 Ibid.
29 Ibid.
30 Alice G. Walton, "New Study Shows How Marijuana's Potency Has
Changed Over Time," *Forbes*, March 23, 2015.
https://www.forbes.com/sites/alicegwalton/2015/03/23/pot-evolution-
how-the-makeup-of-marijuana-has-changed-over-time/#2c5997559e59.
31 Jacob Sullum, "Is Marijuana a Gateway to Opioids?" *Reason, Free
Minds and Free Markets*, April 15, 2019.
https://reason.com/2019/04/15/is-marijuana-a-gateway-to-opioids/
32 John Coleman, *Conspirator's Hierarchy: The Story of the Committee
of 300* (Carson City, Nevada: America West Publishers, 1992).
33 Daily Motion Staff. "Aaron Russo talks about the Rockefeller
Conspiracy," *Daily Motion*, February 2, 2017.
https://www.dailymotion.com/video/x3396yi.
34 Chloe Sorvino, "An Inside Look at The Biggest Drug Reformer in
The Country: George Soros, *Forbes,* October 2, 2014.
https://www.forbes.com/sites/chloesorvino/2014/10/02/an-inside-look-
at-the-biggest-drug-reformer-in-the-country-george-
soros/#818a68b1e295
35 Benjamin Soskis, "George Soros and the Demonization of
Philanthropy," *The Atlantic,* December 5, 2017.
https://www.theatlantic.com/business/archive/2017/12/soros-
philanthropy/547247/.

36 Eric Bailey, "6 Wealthy Donors Aid Measure on Marijuana," *The
Los Angeles Times*, November 2, 1996.
https://www.latimes.com/archives/la-xpm-1996-11-02-mn-60512-
story.html.
37 Ibid.
38 Tyler Durdin, "AG Barr Blasts Soros For Stoking Hatred of Police,"
Zero Hedge, December 22, 2019.
https://www.zerohedge.com/political/ag-barr-slams-soros-funded-
leftist-prosecutors-pursuing-other-social-
agendas?utm_source=feedburner&utm_medium=feed&utm_campaign
=Feed%3A+zerohedge%2Ffeed+%28zero+hedge+-
+on+a+long+enough+timeline%2C+the+survival+rate+for+everyone+
drops+to+zero%29
39 John Coleman, *Conspirator's Hierarchy Story of the Committee of
300* (Carson City, Nevada: America West Publishers, 1992).

40 John Coleman, *The Tavistock Institute Of Human Relations Shaping the Moral, Spiritual, Cultural, and Political and Economic Decline of the United States of America* (Las Vegas, Nevada: World Intelligence Review Publishing, 2006).

41 Ibid.

42 Ibid.

43 Daniel Estulin, Tavistock Institute, Social Engineering the Masses (Walterville, Oregon: Trine Day Publishing, 2015).

44 Ibid.

45 Mining Journal Editorial Board, "Holocaust Survivor's Message Remains Relevant Today," *The Mining Journal*, November 13, 2019. https://www.miningjournal.net/opinion/editorial/2019/11/holocaust-survivors-message-remains-relevant-today/

46 Brian Nugent, *The Toronto Protocol: The Real Plan of the Global Elite?* (Morrisville, North Carolina: Lulu Press, 2018).

47 George Orwell, *Nineteen Eighty-Four* (Westminster, London: Penguin Publishing Group, 1950).

48 Joachim Hagopian, "The Evils of Big Pharma Exposed," *Global Research*, July 19, 2018. https://www.globalresearch.ca/the-evils-of-big-pharma-exposed/5425382.

49 Ibid.

50 Fidel Ruz, "The World Government, Part I," *Monthly Review*, August 17, 2010. https://monthlyreview.org/castro/the-world-government-part-1/.

51 Jim Salter, "Mexican meth increasingly supplanting at-home labs," Monterey Herald, September 14, 2018. https://www.montereyherald.com/2014/11/08/mexican-meth-increasingly-supplanting-at-home-labs/.

52 Mark Perry, "The shocking story behind Richard Nixon's 'War on Drugs' that targeted blacks and anti-war activists." *AEI*, June 14, 2018. https://www.aei.org/carpe-diem/the-shocking-and-sickening-story-behind-nixons-war-on-drugs-that-targeted-blacks-and-anti-war-activists/.

53 Lisa Sacco. "Drug Enforcement in the United States: History, Policy, and Trends," *Congressional Research Service*, October 2, 2014. https://fas.org/sgp/crs/misc/R43749.pdf.

54 History.com Editors, "War on Drugs," *History.com*, December 17, 2019. https://www.history.com/topics/crime/the-war-on-drugs.

55 Nancy Marion, Drugs in American Society: An Encyclopedia of History, Politics, Culture, and the Law (Santa Barbara, California: ABC-CLIO Publishing, 2014).

56 Jeremy Travis, "The Growth of Incarceration in the United States: Exploring Causes and Consequences," *CUNY Academic Works*, 2014.

https://academicworks.cuny.edu/cgi/viewcontent.cgi?article=1026&context=jj_pubs.

57 Ibid.

58On the Issues Staff Writer, "Gerald Ford on Drugs, "*On the Issues*, September 12, 2018. https://www.ontheissues.org/Celeb/Gerald_Ford_Drugs.htm

59 Evan Puschak, "Jimmy Carter says marijuana legalization is A-OK," *MSNBC News*, December 12, 2012. http://www.msnbc.com/the-last-word/jimmy-carter-says-marijuana-legalization

60 Ibid.

61 Gerald Boyd, "Reagan Signs Anti-Drug Measure; Hopes For 'Drug-Free Generation'," *The New York Times*, October 28, 1986. https://www.nytimes.com/1986/10/28/us/reagan-signs-anti-drug-measure-hopes-for-drug-gree-generation.html

62 Ibid.

63 Susanne Karstedt, "Great facts and new facts: The end of U.S. mass imprisonment?" *Cato Unbound*, September 24, 2015. https://www.cato-unbound.org/2015/09/24/susanne-karstedt/great-facts-new-facts-end-us-mass-imprisonment.

64 German Lopez, "A big part of the war on drugs is based on a huge myth," *Vox*, July 10, 2015. https://www.vox.com/2015/7/10/8928421/crack-babies-myth.

65 John Ehrenreich, "Rethinking Incarceration," *The American Prospect*, January 3, 2019. https://prospect.org/justice/rethinking-incarceration/.

66 Arun Gupta, "Let's Talk About George H.W. Bush's Role in the Iran-Contra Scandal," *The Intercept*, December 7, 2018. https://theintercept.com/2018/12/07/george-h-w-bush-iran-contra/

67 Mike Hendrin, "Bush 'Out of These Troubled Times . . . A New World Order'," *News Talk 1290*, November 12, 2013. https://newstalk1290.com/president-bush-1991-the-new-world-order/

68 Matthew Pembleton, "George H.W. Bush's biggest failure? The war on drugs," *The Washington Post*, December 6, 2018. https://www.washingtonpost.com/outlook/2018/12/06/george-hw-bushs-biggest-failure-war-drugs/

69 Ibid.

70 Monica Rohr, "George H.W. Bush leaves mixed record on race, civil rights," *USA Today*, December 3, 2018. https://www.usatoday.com/story/news/2018/12/03/george-h-w-bush-race-civil-rights-war-drugs/2197675002/

71 Linda Mancillas, *Presidents and Mass Incarceration: Choices at the Top, Repercussions at the Bottom* (Santa Barbara, California: ABC-CLIO Publishing, 2018).

72 Medhi Hasan, "The Ignored Legacy of George H.W. Bush: War Crimes, Racism, and Obstruction of Justice," *The Intercept*, December 1, 2018. https://theintercept.com/2018/12/01/the-ignored-legacy-of-george-h-w-bush-war-crimes-racism-and-obstruction-of-justice/?comments=1

73 Daniel Estulin, *Shadow Masters* (Walterville, Oregon: Trine Day Publishing, 2010).

74 David Johnstone, "Bush Pardons 6 in Iran Affair, Aborting a Weinberger Trial; Prosecutor Assails 'Cover-Up'," *The New York Times*, December 25, 1992. https://archive.nytimes.com/www.nytimes.com/books/97/06/29/reviews/iran-pardon.html

75 Medhi Hasan, "The Ignored Legacy of George H.W. Bush: War Crimes, Racism, and Obstruction of Justice," *The Intercept*, December 1, 2018. https://theintercept.com/2018/12/01/the-ignored-legacy-of-george-h-w-bush-war-crimes-racism-and-obstruction-of-justice/?comments=1

76 Micah Morrison, The Mena Coverup," *The Wall Street Journal*, March 3, 1999. https://www.wsj.com/articles/SB920421328276427000.

77 Thomas Frank, "Bill Clinton's crime bill destroyed lives, and there's no point denying it," *The Guardian*, April 15, 2016. https://www.theguardian.com/commentisfree/2016/apr/15/bill-clinton-crime-bill-hillary-black-lives-thomas-frank

78 Donna Murch, "The Clintons' War on Drugs: When Black Lives Didn't Matter," *The New Republic*, February 9, 2016. https://newrepublic.com/article/129433/clintons-war-drugs-black-lives-didnt-matter.

79 Elizabeth Flock, "Bill Clinton, Jimmy Carter Slam War on Drugs in New Documentary," *U.S. News & World Report*, December 3, 2012. https://www.usnews.com/news/blogs/washington-whispers/2012/12/03/bill-clinton-jimmy-carter-slam-war-on-drugs-in-new-documentary

80 Bush, George W., "National Drug Control Strategy," *The White House*, February 2006.

81 On the Issues Staff Writer, "George W. Bush on Drugs," *On the Issues*, September 12, 2018. https://www.ontheissues.org/Celeb/George_W__Bush_Drugs.htm

82 Bush, George W., "National Drug Control Strategy," *The White House*, February 2006.

83 Jeffrey Steinberg, "How Obama Created an Opioid Epidemic," *Pinocchio,* November 4th, 2016.

https://larouchepub.com/eiw/public/2016/eirv43n45-20161104/31-32_4345.pdf.
84Ibid.
85Dara Lind, "One day before he leaves office, Obama just set a record in cutting prisoners' sentences," *Vox*, January 19, 2017. https://www.vox.com/policy-and-politics/2016/11/23/13731448/obama-pardon-clemency-commutation.
86Barbara McQuade, "Smart on Crime Charging Policy Provides Roadmap for More Effective Criminal Justice Strategy," *The University of California Press,* March 30, 2018. https://fsr.ucpress.edu/content/30/3/207.
87German Lopez, "How Obama quietly reshaped America's war on drugs," *Vox*, January 19, 2017. https://www.vox.com/identities/2016/12/19/13903532/obama-war-on-drugs-legacy
88Jeffrey Steinberg, "How Obama Created an Opioid Epidemic," *Pinocchio,* November 4th, 2016. https://larouchepub.com/eiw/public/2016/eirv43n45-20161104/31-32_4345.pdf.
89Hank Berrien, "Obama Tells Border Agents to Stand Down," *The Daily Wire*, February 5, 2016. https://www.dailywire.com/news/obama-tells-border-agents-stand-down-hank-berrien
90John Coleman, *Conspirator's Hierarchy Story of the Committee of 300* (Carson City, Nevada: America West Publishers, 1992).
91Donald Trump, "President Donald J. Trump's Initiative to Stop Opioid Abuse and Reduce Drug Supply and Demand," *The White House Fact Sheet*, March 19, 2018. https://www.whitehouse.gov/briefings-statements/president-donald-j-trumps-initiative-stop-opioid-abuse-reduce-drug-supply-demand/.
92 Greg Allen, "Trump Administration Declares Opioid Crisis A Public Health Emergency," *NPR*, October 26, 2017. https://www.kut.org/post/trump-administration-declare-opioid-crisis-public-health-emergency
93 Ibid.
94Jessica Campisi, "Trump donates third-quarter salary to fight opioid crisis," *The Hill,* November 26, 2019. https://thehill.com/homenews/administration/472027-trump-donates-third-quarter-salary-to-fight-opioid-crisis
95Caroline Halleman, "How Donald Trump's Brother Fred Jr. Shaped His Views on Addiction," Town & Country, October 26, 2017. https://www.townandcountrymag.com/society/politics/a13098008/fred-trump-jr-addiction-history/

96Washington Post Staff Writer, "Trump on his kids: 'No drugs, no alcohol, no cigarettes'," *The Washington Post,* December 1, 2015. https://www.washingtonpost.com/video/national/trump-on-his-kids-no-drugs-no-alcohol-no-cigarettes/2015/12/01/41e1fda0-989b-11e5-aca6-1ae3be6f06d2_video.html.

97Herald-Dispatch Staff, "UPDATE: Melania Trump visits Huntington to learn about opioid epidemic, solutions, *The Huntington Herald-Dispatch,* July 8, 2019. https://www.herald-dispatch.com/_zapp/update-melania-trump-visits-huntington-to-learn-about-opioid-epidemic/article_c70b44c8-a189-11e9-a7cd-a759f0f56ed1.html

98WSJ Staff, "Full Text of President Trump's 2020 State of the Union Speech, *The Wall Street Journal*, February 4, 2020. https://www.wsj.com/articles/full-text-of-president-trumps-2020-state-of-the-union-speech-11580873281.

99J.F., "Why does America have such a big prison population?" *The Economist*, August 15, 2013. https://www.economist.com/the-economist-explains/2013/08/14/why-does-america-have-such-a-big-prison-population

100Jay Stooksberry, "Want to Reduce Gun Violence? Halt the War on Drugs," *Newsweek*, August 16, 2016. https://www.newsweek.com/want-reduce-gun-violence-halt-war-drugs-488879.

101Iserbyt, Charlotte, *The Deliberate Dumbing Down of America: A Chronological Paper Trail* (Ravenna, OH, Conscience Press, 1999).

102Ibid.

103Ibid.

104Churchill, *You and Your Health* (Portland, Maine: J Weston Walch Publishing, 1982).

105Ibid.

106Steph Grob Plante, "If Not D.A.R.E., Then What?" *The Atlantic*, August 28, 2014. https://www.theatlantic.com/health/archive/2014/08/if-not-dare-then-what/376141/

107Katie Jerkovich, "California School District Says Parents Can't Pull Kids Out of New LGBT Sex Ed Class," *The Daily Caller*, April 20, 2018. https://dailycaller.com/2018/04/20/california-school-district-parents-lgbt-sex-ed-mandatory/.

108Iserbyt, Charlotte, *The Deliberate Dumbing Down of America: A Chronological Paper Trail* (Ravenna, OH, Conscience Press, 1999).

109Daniel Estulin, *Shadow Masters* (Walterville, Oregon: Trine Day Publishing, 2010).

110Melissa Block, "Mexican Police Chief Shot and Killed," *NPR*, June 9, 2005. https://www.npr.org/templates/story/story.php?storyId=4696658

111CBS Staff, "U.S.: Mexican drug lord 'world's most powerful'," *CBS News*, January 12, 2012. https://www.cbsnews.com/news/us-mexican-drug-lord-worlds-most-powerful/

112Letzia Paoli, *The Oxford Handbook of Organized Crime* (Oxford, England, U.K.: Oxford University Press, 2014)

113Susan Jones, "DEA: Mexican Criminal Organizations Pose Greatest 'Drug Threat to the United States'," *CNS News*, November 2, 2018. https://www.cnsnews.com/news/article/susan-jones/2018-dea-report-mexico-poses-greatest-criminal-drug-threat-united-states.

114Rebecca Falconer, "Trump vows to designate Mexican drug cartels as terror organizations," *Axios*, November 27, 2019. https://www.axios.com/trump-mexican-drug-cartels-terror-organizations-45b569fd-0816-40a0-9fb3-f153aaf7e6d1.html

115Nikki Carvajal, "Trump to 'temporarily hold off' declaring Mexican cartels terror organizations," *CNN Politics*, December 6, 2019. https://www.cnn.com/2019/12/06/politics/trump-cartels-delay-terror-designation/index.html

116Paul Gootenberg, "Blowback: The Mexican Drug Crisis," *NACLA*, November 18, 2910. https://nacla.org/article/blowback-mexican-drug-crisis

117Daniel Estulin, *Shadow Masters* (Walterville, Oregon: Trine Day Publishing, 2010).

118Nick Gillespie, "How the CIA Turned Us onto LSD and Heroin: Secrets of America's War on Drugs," *Reason*, June 23, 2017. https://reason.com/podcast/anthony-lappe-lsd-heroin-cia-podcast/

119 Ian Tuttle, "El Chapo's Capture Puts 'Operation Fast and Furious' Back in the Headlines." *The National Review*, January 22, 2016. https://www.nationalreview.com/2016/01/fast-furious-obama-first-scandal

120 Ibid.

121 Alex Newman, "Reports: CIA Working with Mexican Drug Cartels," *New American*, August 15, 2011. https://www.thenewamerican.com/world-news/north-america/item/10658-reports-cia-working-with-mexican-drug-cartels.

122 Michael Musalek, "Reduction of harmful consumption versus total abstinence in addiction treatment," *Journal of Neuropsychiatry*, 2013, 3(6). http://www.jneuropsychiatry.org/peer-review/reduction-of-harmful-consumption-versus-total-abstinence-in-addiction-treatment-neuropsychiatry.pdf

123 Stephanie Kim, "At D.A.R.E. graduation, Kendall students pledge to be drug free," *The Hour*, June 13, 2018. https://www.thehour.com/news/article/At-D-A-R-E-graduation-Kendall-students-pledge-12992038.php

124 Naina Bajekal, "Want to Win the War on Drugs? Portugal Might Have the Answer," Time, August 1, 2008. https://time.com/longform/portugal-drug-use-decriminalization/.

125 Katya Sedgwick, "The San Francisco Mess Proves Legalizing Drugs Doesn't Work." *The Federalist*, January 21, 2020. https://thefederalist.com/2020/01/21/the-san-francisco-mess-proves-decriminalizing-drugs-doesnt-work/.

126 Naina Bajekal, "Want to Win the War on Drugs? Portugal Might Have the Answer," Time, August 1, 2008. https://time.com/longform/portugal-drug-use-decriminalization/.

127Elena Gordon, "What's the Evidence That Supervised Drug Injection Sites Save Lives?" *NPR*, September 7, 2018. https://www.npr.org/sections/health-shots/2018/09/07/645609248/whats-the-evidence-that-supervised-drug-injection-sites-save-lives.

128 F. Faggiano, "School-based Prevention for Illicit Drug Use," *Cochrane Library*, December 1, 2014. https://www.cochrane.org/CD003020/ADDICTN_school-based-prevention-illicit-drug-use.

129 Ibid.

130 Max Menius, "The Difference Between Methadone and Suboxone," *Alcohol and Drug Services*, September 21, 2017. https://adsyes.org/addiction-recovery/the-difference-between-methadone-and-suboxone/

131 Ira Mintzer, "Treating Opioid Addiction with Buprenorphine-Naloxone in Community-Based Primary Care Settings," Annals of Family Medicine, March 1, 2017. http://www.annfammed.org/content/5/2/146.full.